Historic Ranches of Texas

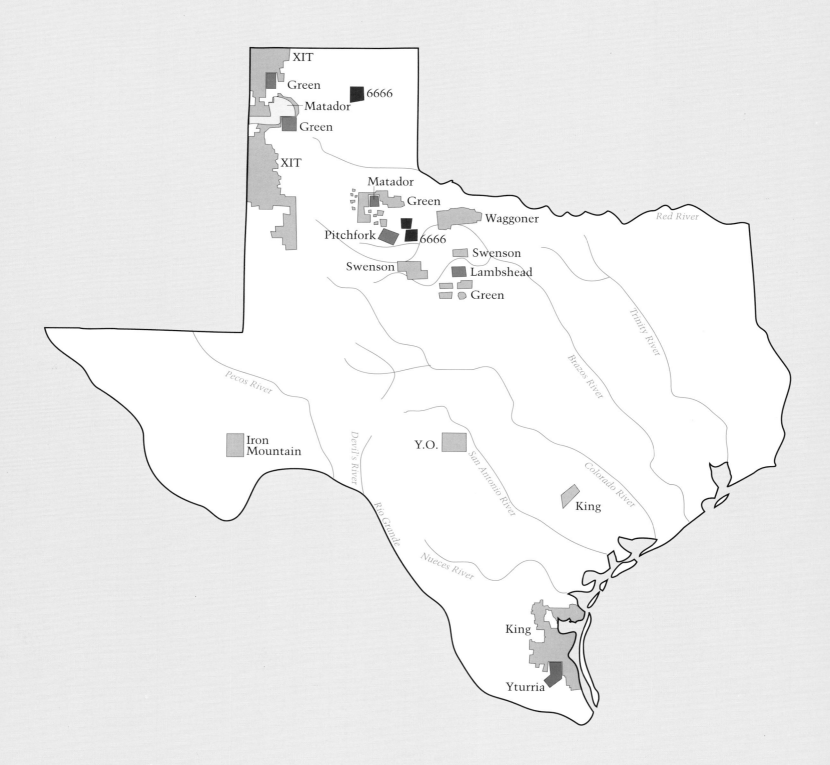

XIT

Green

Matador

Green

6666

XIT

Matador

Green

Waggoner

Pitchfork

6666

Swenson

Swenson

Lambshead

Green

Iron
Mountain

Y.O.

King

King

Yturria

Red River

Trinity River

Brazos River

Pecos River

Devil's River

Rio Grande

San Antonio River

Colorado River

Nueces River

HISTORIC RANCHES OF TEXAS

Text by Lawrence Clayton   Paintings by J. U. Salvant

UNIVERSITY OF TEXAS PRESS, AUSTIN

Copyright © 1993 by the University of Texas Press

All rights reserved

Printed in Hong Kong

First paperback printing, 1997

Requests for permission to reproduce material from this work should be sent to Permissions, University of Texas Press, Box 7819, Austin, TX 78713-7819.

㊾ The paper used in this publication meets the minimum requirements of American National Standard for Information Sciences—Permanence of Paper for Printed Library Materials, ANSI Z39.48-1984.

The color reproductions in this book were made possible through the generous assistance of Burnett Ranches, Inc.

Library of Congress Cataloging-in-Publication Data

Clayton, Lawrence, date
    Historic ranches of Texas / text by Lawrence Clayton :
paintings by J. U. Salvant. — 1st ed.
        p.   cm.
    Includes bibliographical references (p.   ).
    ISBN 0-292-71189-1 (pbk. : alk. paper)
    1. Ranches—Texas.   2. Ranch life—Texas—History.
3. Texas—History, Local.   I. Salvant, J. U. (Joan Usner), date.   II. Title.
F387.C53   1993
976.4'009734—dc20   92-43918

Contents

This book is dedicated
to Sonja Irwin Clayton,
to Texas ranching culture,

and
to Nicholas Gregory Youngblood
and
Benjamin John Youngblood,
first generation of the Salvant family
who can lay claim to the title
Native Texan.

Acknowledgments

I want to express appreciation to the following individuals, who have read parts of the manuscript or provided helpful suggestions or interviews: Dr. David Murrah of the Southwest Collection at Texas Tech University; Dr. Kenneth Davis of Texas Tech University; Buster McLaury of Alanreed; John Stevens of Matador; Gary Mathis of Stamford; Watt Matthews of Albany; the staffs at the Panhandle-Plains Museum in Canyon, the Barker Historical Center in Austin, and the Richardson Library and Research Center of the Southwest at Hardin-Simmons University; Bruce Cheeseman of the King Ranch Archives in Kingsville; J. J. Gibson of the Four Sixes Ranch of Guthrie; Bob and Bill Green of Albany; Charles Schreiner III of Mountain Home; Bill Blakemore II of Midland; Frank Yturria of Brownsville; Leonard Stiles of Kingsville; and Jim Patterson of Electra.

I also wish to express appreciation for the continuing support of my wife, Sonja, and to my two daughters, DeLys Mitchell and Lea Clayton.

—Lawrence Clayton

Information on the ranches and their history was provided by the following people and institutions: J. J. Gibson, ranch manager, 6666 Ranch; Bob and Nancy Green, Green ranches; Bill Blakemore II, Lloyd Stuessy, Pless Stuessy, and Mr. and Mrs. Woodrow Mills, Iron Mountain Ranch; Leonard Stiles (retired Santa Gertrudis Division manager), Bruce Cheeseman (archivist), and Tio Kleberg, King Ranch; Watt Matthews and Mary Featherstone, Lambshead Ranch; Dale Baumgardner (manager) and John Stevens, Matador Ranch; Bob Morehouse (foreman), Pitchfork Ranch; Gary Mathis and Eugene Swenson, Swenson Ranch; Jim Smith, Jim Patterson, and Bucky Wharton, Waggoner Ranch; Ken May, Scarbauer Cattle Company (old XIT Ranch); Charles Schreiner III, Y. O. Ranch; Lydia Yturria Butler and Frank and Mary Yturria, Yturria Ranch; Alvin Davis, Ranching Heritage Museum, Lubbock; Byron Price, Director, Cowboy Hall of Fame, Oklahoma City; Don King, Executive Secretary, Texas and Southwest Cattle Raisers Association; Jim Matthews, Southwest Collection, Archives of the American Southwest, Texas Tech University, Lubbock; and Joan Farmer, Old Jail Art Museum, Albany.

Further information was obtained from the following publications: *Interwoven*, by Sallie Reynolds Matthews; *Lambshead before Interwoven*, by Frances Mayhugh Holden; *Shootout at Squyre's Chapel*, by John Ayres (student publication); "The Long Road," by Willie Weaver Green (memoirs); *The Matador Land and Cattle Company*, by W. M. Pearce; *The Pitchfork Land and Cattle Company*, by David J. Murrah; *SMS Ranches*; "SMS Ranches," in *Handbook of Texas*; *Brave Men and Cold Steel*, by Doug Perkins and Nancy Ward; "Channing Couple Restoring Old XIT General Office," *Amarillo Daily News* (June 11, 1990); *6000 Miles of Fence*, by Cordia Sloan Duke and Joe B. Frantz; *Long Days and Short Nights*, by Neal Barrett, Jr.; *Rip Ford's Texas*, by John Salmon Ford.

The following have been of considerable assistance in the creation of this book: Mr. and Mrs. Henry Musselman, Mr. and Mrs. Austin McCloud, Mr. Stan Cobbs, Mr. and Mrs. Tom Green, Dr. and Mrs. Charles LeMaistre, Dr. David Bowen, Mr. and Mrs. Lester Clark, Mr. and Mrs. C. A. Wilkins, and my husband, Dr. Edwin T. Salvant, Jr., who devoted much of his vacation time to accompany me around Texas to visit all the ranches, critiqued the paintings, proofed and typed the copy for them, encouraged and supported my efforts, and made this project a most enjoyable one.

—J. U. Salvant

Introduction

An aura of romance clings, even in the present time, to the ranching tradition of the American West. Perhaps nowhere is that notion stronger than in Texas, where ranching as we know it today in the United States developed, as did cowboys, those legendary, almost mythic, figures to whom ranching gave a reason to be. The cowboy has dominated the fiction and film depicting the cattle business in Texas— for ranching is basically cattle ranching in the minds of most observers despite large numbers of sheep, goats, and horses on the ranges. For the astute men and women to whom raising cattle to feed a beef-hungry population is a business, cowboying is only part of that life. In some cases ranching may have become a passion pursued despite monetary loss, but the long-lasting ranches survived because smart managers utilized sound business practices. Often a single generation has contended with many factors, climatic as well as economic. Especially is this true of long-lived ranches, for many an operation has gone broke after a decade or two because of drought, glutted markets, low prices, or poor management.

Ranches that have survived over several generations have done so only because of several fortuitous conditions. Perhaps primary is the availability of resources to continue the operation. Money from oil often provided that necessity and allowed the ranch to survive. But equally as crucial to the survival of a ranch is a family member both able and willing to take on the demanding job of managing the affairs of the ranch. Vision for the future and ranching sense to handle the present are two important assets not always found in the children of ranchers. It may be one or more of the grandchildren who have taken up the task. Often children raised on the ranch see only the hard work, isolation, and loneliness. When succession skips a generation, however, a grandchild who may have visited the ranch only periodically but still has the capacity to be a successful ranch manager may take up the task. It is not uncommon for children to inherit a ranch and sell it or be forced to sell part of

it to pay the inheritance taxes. More than one has lost the family fortune through ill-advised investments. The future is always a matter of concern for a ranching family.

When one thinks of great ranches, one often thinks of successful ranching families, and family names loom large in the history of these sometimes enormous spreads of land that stretched, in earlier days, to a million acres or more. Such names as Kleberg, King, Burnett, Swenson, Schreiner, Slaughter, Scharbaugh, Goodnight, Adair, Waggoner, Reynolds, Matthews, and others stand as great ranching names in Texas. And for good reasons. These names represent families that put together, and weathered hard times to hold together, enormous tracts of property on which were raised quality cattle and horses and, in marginal areas, sheep and goats. Ranchers promoted the features of one breed, or some particular crossing of breeds, to develop cattle adapted to ranges in a given area. In one case, a ranch developed its own breed. The offspring of famous Quarter Horse bloodlines associated with ranches have graced roping arenas, cutting pens, and race tracks, but, more important, they have provided cowboys the best horses available to work cattle in the sometimes huge pastures on these ranches.

Several consistent factors crop up in the stories of ranches that survive. One of these is the vision of the founder. Charles Schreiner saw a dream in the Texas Hill Country; young William Henry Green saw his future in an eight-thousand-acre stretch of well-watered open range along Hubbard Creek; or a board member or director of a corporation had a view of a ranching empire in Texas. Often someone with shrewd business sense saw the chance to make a fortune and brought the notion to reality.

Another key factor was money to establish the operation. A fortune eventually might be generated by the investment, but unless the rancher started in a modest way, a small fortune could be required to begin—to control or later buy the range, to purchase stock, to hire men, to build fences and corrals and houses and barns, to wait for the herd to multiply and the calves to grow to marketing size, and then to get the animals to market at a time when the price was the best possible to produce a positive financial return.

The stories of the sources of this money are interesting to pursue. Some of it came from outside the United States. For example, an investment group from Scotland provided the money for the Matador. As much as thirty million dollars of foreign capital, mostly from England and Scotland, was invested between 1875 and 1885. In other cases the money flowed from commerce and finance within the United States. Schreiner and Swenson generated their money from the mercantile and business world. The construction of the state capitol in Austin provided the financial impetus for the XIT. Judge J. A. Matthews gained his backing by forming his own investment group of local men and using their money to purchase cattle to populate the vast ranges he already controlled. Later the land and cattle were divided among the investors. The Greens wrested their resources from the land itself by hard work and frugality. Each ranch has a similar but somewhat different origin.

Oil production later had a huge impact on success. Texas oil millionaires became legendary, a breed apart from financial tycoons in other states. And with good reason. When Texas joined the Union, it retained private ownership of most of the land and the minerals beneath it, all the way down to the earth's core. Unlike many other western states, Texas has no vast tracts of public lands managed by the Bureau of Land Management. State and federal parks are the closest to that found here. This oil production funded more than one ranching operation in Texas, for there is definitely a strong link between oil wealth and successful ranching. "Black gold" sometimes provides money for acquisition of land and livestock as well as improvements on that land, and oil makes surviving at ranching a much more achievable goal.

Lack of water and a paucity of suitable forage were problems that all ranchers had to overcome. The vast stretches of semi-arid and poorly watered lands could support some livestock, but water within easy walking distance is essential for productive livestock operations.

Finding cattle suitable for the range of a given ranch was also a problem. The King Ranch developed its own with Brahma imported from India to crossbreed. Others settled on a line of Herefords. Most eventually rejected the other prominent choice of British breeds of that day, the Durham or shorthorn, and later the Angus breed found widespread favor. These British breeds were first crossbred with Longhorn stock by necessity because only bulls were imported at first. Later other breeds came along—Charolais, Limousin, and even Japanese breeds. But most ranchers still prefer at least some reliance on the British breeds, mainly Hereford. A common cross these days is a balance of Hereford, Angus, and Brahma, but Longhorn blood is still evident; especially will the mottled hides of part-Longhorn herds be seen as the result of breeding Longhorn bulls to first-calf heifers. Some ranches find the offspring make hearty, thrifty range cows, which when bred to Hereford bulls provide a one-fourth Longhorn calf with classic Hereford markings, large frame, and excellent beef potential.

The problems to be solved often were beyond the reach of individual ranchers, and solutions had to come from outside, perhaps from another rancher. The King Ranch personnel are sometimes credited with the discovery that Texas fever, a mysterious but deadly disease, was caused by a tick and that dipping stock in insecticide-laced water in a cement or stone vat was the solution. The practice became widely established, and a potentially disastrous situation that caused anger, frustration, and fear disappeared.

Some animals indigenous to the West created problems. Prairie dogs, small mammals that yelp like a dog, burrowed holes into the prairies, creating hazards that could be fatal to a horse and rider. The creatures ate huge amounts of grass, and their tunnels caused water to run into the ground rather than spread over the surface to nourish the grass or fill tanks. Range freed from the pests supported from 10 percent to 25 percent more cattle, and ranchers undertook eradication programs with a vengeance. Wolves and coyotes also were a menace. Wolves were especially destructive because they could hamstring a large animal and then devour it. A bounty system encouraged their elimination. Coyotes, despite the romance sometimes associated with them, are still a hazard to small animals, especially calves, sheep, goats, and some game birds. These creatures have adapted to modern life in a remarkable way.

Medical problems included the fatal black leg, for which a vaccine must be administered to young calves; stomach worms; grubs; dwarfism in Hereford cattle; and screwworms. Perhaps no single other factor changed life on a ranch as did eliminating the screwworm, for doctoring calves for the life-threatening worms caused the cattle to be wild and kept cowboys on the prowl in pastures in the warm months. Brucellosis threatened the industry but was controlled. Uncontrolled, almost any one of these diseases would have ended ranching as we know it. Other diseases continue to threaten, such as antiplasmosis and leptospirosis, diseases that cause cows to abort their fetuses and for which ranchers must vaccinate.

Contemporary problems may be solved with old solutions. The high cost of gasoline and equipment may bring back the chuck wagon to save on fuel, pickups, trailers, and the like. We may once again see mules and work horses become even more popular than in recent years when their use has been growing. New wagons are being produced now because of the demand by wagon clubs and trail riding groups. One wonders if the cowboys will adjust to spending time out on the wagon as their predecessors did. If they are true cowboys, they will do it. And then the question arises of whether the wives can adjust, or will cowboys be once again forced into bachelorhood. Working this way will require more men and more horses on large ranches. We may once again see many ranches getting out the Dutch ovens

and soogans, or bedrolls, and loading the wagons twice a year for work on the range. This development may encourage forming smaller ranches with less distance to cover, and in that way the spreads will be more manageable.

Size is important in a ranch. From the King Ranch's present-day vast stretches of over 800,000 acres and the Waggoner's 500,000 acres, even these contemporary ranches seem dwarfed by the three million acres of the glory days of the XIT and the Matador. The minimum size to deserve the label "ranch" varies from region to region, depending principally upon rainfall and quality of soil. In East Texas, where the rich creek and river bottoms may support a cow per acre in the lush growing seasons, a ranch may have only a few hundred acres and still support a sizable herd of livestock. In some parts of West Texas, near Albany, for example, a minimum of ten thousand acres is needed for a suitable operation, for a cow needs twenty to twenty-five acres to find sufficient grazing. In far West Texas it may take three or four times that many acres per cow.

A ranch today will typically have a horse pasture, often one pasture reserved for holding cattle gathered at shipping time, and ample pastures to run the herd of several hundred to several thousand mother cows and/or steers, numbers sufficient to generate enough income to pay the expense of the operation. Across the large ranches are camps. Each usually has a house with a set of pens, a horse pasture, and a feed house. Here a cowboy and his family live so that he can look after the stock in the pastures near the house and feed them during the winter. He also carefully watches the availability of forage for the stock and monitors precious rainfall.

During the open-range period, cattle grazed on grass growing on the finest soil the state could offer, from the well-watered coastal plains to the deep soils of the Texas high plains. With the discovery of irrigation water on the high plains, population density became greater, and the best land was sold off and put into cultivation or otherwise removed from grazing. Then cattle were forced to marginal land with shallow soil, too much change in elevation for plowing, or too stony for growing crops. This kind of land is good for little else than grazing livestock or providing habitat for wild game. These open spaces are apt to remain in such use because of geologic features and rainfall insufficient to support dense populations of people. Hundreds of large ranches in existence for decades, some for more than a hundred years, are scattered over the less populous areas of the state, particularly from the brushy South Texas plains, in the portion of Texas west of Fort Worth, and in the northern Panhandle. Many of these are viable working operations maintaining the ranching traditions of Texas.

Name changes connected with the various ranches occur when ranch daughters marry. Ranching families often unite in this way to form larger ranching empires, which are later split among descendants. But the family line will have the orientation and resources to continue to expand and contract to fit the markets and land available by sale or lease. It is fortunate that these families continue in the ranching business. Founding new ranch dynasties today is unlikely because of the difficulty of financing. This inaccessibility makes ranching even more exotic and desirable to many of us.

The sketches in this book present several prominent ranches in Texas both large and small, comparatively speaking, as well as some no longer in business as the original organization. The format resembles J. Evetts Haley's excellent book *The Heraldry of the Range*, a study including seven ranches, two of which are included here—the XIT and Matador. Certainly not all the historic ranches in Texas and the Southwest are in the present collection, either.

Several factors influenced selection of these ranches. Recognizable name was one. Geographic distribution was also a consideration so as to reflect ranching practices from various parts of the state. Availability of resources or the willingness of ranch owners to cooperate posed a limiting factor and caused inclusion of some and exclusion of others. With these items in mind, J. U. Salvant and I, with the help of Frankie Westbrook, our editor at the University of Texas Press, queried various people about possible candidates for inclusion. The list originally contained some twenty entries of ranches or categories for ranches, such as "Spanish-influenced operation," and other such criteria. We then prepared a list of those that just could not be excluded from a look at major historic Texas ranches. The XIT was at the top of the list and remained despite its demise decades ago. It also serves as an example that even in Texas something can be "too big." The relationship of the ranch to the state capitol also argued for its inclusion. The Matador, because of its relationship with foreign investors, made the final list even though the ranch currently operated under its name is but a shadow of the former giant spread across the western and northern parts of Texas. The Y.O.'s current operation and diversity, especially its reputation for exotic game and its lack of oil resources, argued for its place on the list. The King Ranch, still a viable ranching and farming operation, is too integral a part of the Texas ranching picture to be excluded. It is the only one to develop its own breed of cattle.

The four ranches across the northern part of the state— Waggoner, Four Sixes, Pitchfork, and Swenson, not widely separated geographically—have colorful but quite different stories and have experienced different fortunes. They were far too prominent to ignore.

The Matthews and Green ranches, quite close together in location, nonetheless have diverse development and represent a pocket of ranching culture still strong and vibrant.

The Yturria Ranch represents one of the ranches still belonging to the Spanish heritage to which all of Texas ranching owes its roots, and one of the current owners graciously consented to be included.

Iron Mountain Ranch serves as an example of ranching in the Big Bend area and is only one of several in that particularly rich ranching region.

Written material on some of these ranches is available, as a check of the bibliography will show. Others, however, have little or no printed histories at all. The stories of the Yturria, Iron Mountain, and Green are not well documented, but they have faithful admirers who have preserved the stories and are willing to make the information available for print. In no case were the contemporary details available from printed sources. This information came from people familiar with the operation of the ranch in question.

At least as interesting as why some ranches are here is why others are not. In some cases the ranch was not included because its story seemed much like one or more already included. In other cases ranchers opted not to be included for personal reasons. Owners of other ranches felt they wanted to retain their own stories for their own use. Others were not included because of lack of space. We hope that other volumes will make up this deficiency.

Included for each ranch, where the information is available, are details of the location, the founding, the growth from the original days to the present, the individuals who figured prominently in the development of the ranch, the amount of land included, the brands associated with the ranch, the breeds of cattle, and the bloodlines of the horses.

Each ranch is represented artistically by the paintings of Joan Salvant. Her watercolors represent landmarks particularly important to the heritage of the ranch. Each painting embodies the essence or spirit of that ranch in a way that can be achieved only through art, where one can feel the underlying reality and romance that have come to be associated with that spread.

In conclusion, those readers searching for a revisionist text to debunk the admittedly often romanticized view of ranching will need to look elsewhere. I have tried to make the points about each ranch clearly and to support the statements either from printed texts or from interviews, and I hope I have succeeded in not being sentimental. But this is not an effort in revisionist history. I strove for a middle of the road depiction based on the facts and interpretation as well as on my own views.

—Near Old Fort Griffin on the Clear Fork of the Brazos

Artist's Notes

To one who was born and reared in a large metropolitan area (where the only place to see live animals other than my cat or the neighbor's dog was the zoo), this has been two years of tremendous enlightenment and exposure to a new and exciting segment of life. As I reflect on my experience, the first mental pictures are of people who acquainted me with the myriad aspects of ranch life, both past and present.

To the ranch managers and owners who took time from their very busy schedule to escort my husband and me around, I owe a great deal. Their warm Texas hospitality was most appreciated. They drove me over their vast ranches, sometimes over roads but more often across rocky cactus-filled fields and down into the boulder-strewn creeks and river beds to show me the vastness of the cattle industry and the roots of their rich heritage. One such experience resulted in a tire blowout and the discovery that we had no tire jack and were fifteen miles from headquarters. But totally unflappable Charles Schreiner III used his car radio to summon help. While we waited I took the opportunity to sketch the lovely surroundings. Presently, a 300-pound man drove up, and in what seemed only seconds the tire was changed and we were on our way once again.

A deep sense of gratitude goes to those who feel that preserving our past is important for future generations and have taken strides to restore it. I found that people on all the ranches I visited feel this way, but King, Lambshead, Y. O., and Yturria have done extensive restoration and preservation on their own, and the Ranching Heritage Museum in Lubbock is dedicated to that end.

I am especially grateful to those pioneer ranchers who endured drought, disease, hurricanes, tornadoes, dust storms, and endless years of difficult work but never lost faith in God, the land, or themselves and developed this marvelous land of Texas. What a legacy they have handed down to us.

One group of people who deserve special recognition are the cowboys. Without them all this never would have been. For all their rough nature, they seem to be a most polite and gentlemanly group. How refreshing to have the door opened for me, to see them stand and remove their hats when a woman entered the room. Yet it was not a chauvinistic attitude but respect for someone different in abilities and background. It was a pleasure to share time with them.

All in all, it has been a time that has enlightened me and stretched my abilities as an artist. Those who have seen the original paintings are surprised to see so many horses, cattle, and people as well as the familiar buildings I normally choose as subjects. Some of the time during the two years spent to complete these paintings was devoted to the study of cattle breeds and horse flesh in order to realistically represent them in the paintings. I hope I have not fallen too short. Some paintings, you will note, are placed back in time while others are of ranching as it is today. Two of the paintings—the King Ranch hacienda and the Lutheran church on Swenson Ranch—speak of both yesterday and today. Some subjects exist today while others are only memories, as in Roaring Springs on Matador, the XIT stage stop, Bethel Chapel on Green Ranch, and Iron Mountain.

Most of all I say thank you to my coauthor, Dr. Lawrence Clayton, whose knowledge of cowboys and the history of ranching is, in my opinion, unsurpassed. He opened many doors to new acquaintances as well as doors of understanding of the subject treated in this book.

My hope is that the readers will enjoy this book as much as the authors enjoyed creating it.

Historic Ranches of Texas

Four Sixes Ranch (6666)

Headquarters at Guthrie

One of the most famous stories about the founding of a ranch involves the Four Sixes. Legend has it that a cowman named Burk Burnett was in a high stakes card game. One of the players had lost all of his money but was determined to push on. All he had left to bet was a large ranch in West Texas. Burk played for the ranch and won with a hand consisting of four sixes, hence the name of the ranch.

The only problem with the story is that it probably is not true. At least Burk Burnett, the principal figure in the tale and one of the giants of Texas ranching, repeatedly denied the authenticity of the story. But the romance associated with the Four Sixes Ranch, whose headquarters is located near Guthrie in northwestern Texas, has nonetheless continued to flourish for nearly a hundred years. The source of the brand was not the card game but likely came to be associated with the ranch because of a herd of cattle that Burnett bought near Denton, Texas. The animals already wore the Four Sixes brand, which Burnett continued to use.

Burk Burnett came from Bates County, Missouri, where he was born on January 1, 1849. After outlaws burned his family home, the family moved to Texas. Burnett went to work as a cowboy in 1868, just as the glory days of trail driving got underway, by joining an outfit headed to Abilene, Kansas, over the Chisholm Trail. The next year he took a family herd up the trail, but this trip proved disastrous. Indians ran off most of the horse herd, leaving each man with only the horse he was riding at the time of the raid. Burnett did not have the funds to buy additional mounts, even if he could have found them. He instructed each man to walk after the herd all day and to ride his horse only at night. In this manner the crew finally brought the herd to market. Because of the way he performed on this trip, Burnett became a partner with his father and thereby became a rancher instead of remaining a cowboy.

The Burnetts first ranched in the area where the city of Wichita Falls now stands and also leased extensive tracts in Indian Territory, now the state of Oklahoma, across the Red River. When government regulations and settlement took away access to these grasslands, Burnett saw he would have to buy more land. He bought the present Four Sixes headquarters in 1900 from the Louisville Land and Cattle Company, and thus began the real legend of the Four Sixes. Among his many contributions was helping found the Northwest Texas Stock Raisers Association at Graham in 1877. He also once hosted newly inaugurated President Theodore Roosevelt on a wolf hunt on the grasslands in Indian Territory.

The elder Burnett died in 1922, and control of the ranch passed to his son Tom, who had established the Triangle ranches to the northeast of his father's property. Burk, however, is remembered for many reasons, principally through the name of a town laid out on a new railroad line near Wichita Falls; the town, still in existence, was appropriately dubbed Burkburnett and stands on the original ranch property of the Burnetts. The ranch has continued to be run by descendants of the original Burnetts, because Tom was followed by his daughter Anne Tandy, who in turn was followed by her daughter Anne Burnett Marion, the current owner. Many Texas ranches lie away from public thoroughfares, but this is not the case with the Four Sixes. The main rock house built in 1917 at a cost of $100,000 is plainly visible from U.S. Highway 83, a short distance northwest of Guthrie. The house has oak floors, maple paneling, and other attributes of a fine house. The renovation and redecoration of the structure are the subject of an article in *Architectural Digest*. Located adjacent to the house are a large bunkhouse, a ranch store, and other buildings constructed of stone.

Many people think of the Four Sixes as being the Guthrie property only, but the ranch was at one time composed of four divisions comprising nearly a half million acres: 208,000 acres at Guthrie; 108,000 acres on the Triangle

Ranch near Paducah; 30,000 acres on the Triangle Ranch near Iowa Park; and 108,000 acres on Dixon Creek between Borger and Panhandle. The ranges are cut into pastures ranging from 7,000 to 15,000 acres. Recent acquisitions include the 10,000-acre Kincaid Ranch, which Anne Marion bought in order to consolidate part of the Triangle properties, and about fifty sections of the old JY Ranch, east of the 6666. The Triangle Ranch at Iowa Park has been sold.

The ranch history includes some problem with Indians. Burk Burnett and W. T. Waggoner, owner of the famous Waggoner Ranch, like Charles Goodnight did much to cultivate friendships with Indians. Burnett and Waggoner once invited Yellow Bear and Quanah Parker, well-known Comanche chiefs, to accompany them to Fort Worth to a social gathering. In his hotel room when he went to bed, Yellow Bear simply blew out the gas light, as he would have a kerosene lamp, and died from asphyxiation. Indians in the tribe felt that the death was due to underhanded means until Burnett took two bottles of ammonia to the Indians and let them smell "bad air" that could bring about a man's death.

The ranch has been fortunate to have three talented managers. The first was Bud Arnett. Arnett's story is unique in that he was the manager of the same piece of property for more than fifty years, even though the property was owned by three different companies. He began to manage some of the property when it was owned by Sam J. Lazarus and later by the Louisville Land and Cattle Company in the early 1880s. When Burk Burnett later bought the property, Arnett stayed on and became legendary in his role as boss of the cowboys on the ranch. Arnett remained with this work until he was replaced by Horace Bryant, son of the wagon boss on the neighboring Pitchfork Ranch. Bryant was also Arnett's son-in-law. Bryant stayed with the job only two years before moving on.

In 1932, however, another legendary figure appeared on the scene: George Humphreys, long-time manager, whose tenure ran from 1932 until 1970. George's father, John, had refused a job offered by Burk Burnett in 1899. When Burnett showed him the wild horses that would be in his string, John drifted on south and began ranching on his own. George's mother died, however, when the boy was nine days old, and George was raised by a family friend until he was two years of age and then returned to live with his father. At age fifteen, however, because he could not get along with his stepmother, George quit school and took his first ranch job. It was not long afterward that he took a job with the Four Sixes breaking broncs. Thus began a career that spanned fifty-two years. George soon married and moved to the ranch's North Camp in 1925, but in 1926 he moved to the headquarters at Guthrie. For many years he joined the cowboys, whose home for much of the time was a chuck wagon that was moved around the ranch to where the work was being done. When King County needed a new sheriff, George sensed the call and was elected sheriff in 1928, but he continued his cowboying duties. George retired at age seventy in 1970 and moved to his ranch in Stonewall County, south of Aspermont, which he and his wife had been preparing for their retirement for many years.

The current manager is J. J. Gibson. His role in running the ranch has been significant, and he has helped turn it into a modern operation. When the manager of the Triangle ranches quit, Gibson assumed control of both, and now he oversees all of the sprawling ranges. Gibson, the youngest of nine children, is the product of Texas ranch land. His grandparents came to Young County in Texas after the Civil War. J. J.'s father worked as a cowboy for the old Louisville Land and Cattle Company. After Gibson's father married the local schoolteacher, Emma Merrick, in 1898, the couple founded their own ranch that bordered the Four Sixes on the northeast, on the line between Cottle and King counties near Paducah, where J. J. later graduated from high school. Gibson served in the U.S. Marine Corps during World War

II in the Pacific campaign and participated in the fierce fighting at Guadalcanal and Okinawa. He returned home after the war, finished his degree at Texas Christian University, and took the job offered by manager George Humphreys to come to the Four Sixes Ranch. He has been there in positions of responsibility ever since. In 1948, he married Naida Richards, daughter of a pioneer ranching family from the Paducah area. They have two sons, Jim and Mike.

The Four Sixes Ranch is famous for its high-quality Hereford cattle, and more than seven thousand cows still range on the Guthrie ranch alone. Gibson has encouraged crossbreeding, and some two thousand cows crossed with Brangus blood roam on the home ranch, as well as others at the Triangle at Paducah. The Dixon Creek ranges yearlings from the other three divisions until the animals are ready for the feed lot. All steers and heifers not kept for replacements are finished in the feed lot and sold to packers. The 6666 was one of the first to feed its own yearlings for market. The ranch still calves between thirteen hundred and fourteen hundred heifers a year and has just over twenty employees. These live in five camps on the home ranch and scattered across the other divisions as need demands. In the 1930s the chuck wagon and its crew stayed out from April to June, and again from September to December, to accommodate the two seasonal working periods on the ranch. Today those periods have been pushed back. The branding period starts in early February, if possible, and the wagon rolls out by mid-March and stays out until around the first of May. A crew of fourteen men usually works off the wagon these days. When working the Triangle ranges, four to six more men who live in camps on the ranch may augment the crew. The summer and fall work begins after July 4 and ends in the late summer. The calves are roped and dragged, a procedure that many cowboys feel is the easiest on the cattle, easiest on the men, and the fastest way to accomplish the work. The men still separate the cows and calves in pens by putting two men in the gate and having mounted riders push cows and calves toward the gate. The calves are cut back and the cows are allowed to go through. The cutting alley, a long narrow section of the pen with gates opening into other pens, is not used on the Four Sixes.

Horses have long played an important role at the Four Sixes Ranch. Burk Burnett himself bought some quality horses from the Comanche herd of Quanah Parker. Years later, when the planning meeting that resulted in the formation of the American Quarter Horse Association was held, it was in the Fort Worth home of Jim and Ann Burnett Hall, in November of 1940. Burnetts have usually been serious about their horses, but in the 1930s when John Burns took over as manager, he found only twenty-eight mares in the breeding herd. He soon bought twenty more, which came from stock of the Graham brothers of Lovington, New Mexico. Burns was joined in the dream of building a horse herd by George Humphreys, whose love of good horses equaled that of Burns. From that time on, a long line of famous stallions have been used on the band of brood mares. In the mid-1930s, a gray stallion named Tom or Scooter, a former race horse with some Arabian blood but with classic Quarter Horse conformation, was used. Buggins, a bay Thoroughbred, also ran with the mare band. Another Thoroughbred stallion was King O'Neill II; later, other stallions include Salty Chief, Joe Tom, and Rainy Day.

George Humphreys spotted a colt that became famous as Hollywood Gold, a dun stallion that had excellent capabilities in the cutting arena. Humphreys also made a wise move when he brought in Cee Bar, a horse with some Thoroughbred blood, which was used on the ranch for about seven years.

In the 1940s, 175 saddle horses made up the remuda at the Four Sixes. Today the mare band runs just under a hundred. No geldings are sold, though extra fillies are often sold off. The gentling method made famous by the widely

CHUCK WAGON TENT

This ranch was visited by the artist at spring roundup time and the weather turned bitter cold. We dined at the chuck wagon under an enclosed tent—very warm and cozy. These wranglers were a most polite group of gentlemen and I was made to feel very welcome. Notice the "cowboy crystal"—coffee cans used for a large quantity of tea to complement a hearty meal of beef and gravy, potatoes, beans, and that wonderful peach cobbler that cook Joe Propps makes so well.

THE COMPANY STORE AND RANCH HEADQUARTERS

Most ranch headquarters seem to be located far away from population centers, but not so on the Four Sixes Ranch. It is located on a gentle rise just northwest of the town of Guthrie at the intersection of U.S. Highways 82 and 83. Guthrie consists of only a few homes and buildings, including the courthouse for King County and the Four Sixes supply house, or commissary. The supply house is the oldest structure standing that was built by Burk Burnett. In the painting can be seen the main house on the rise, some cowboy residences, and the Four Sixes barn made famous in many Marlboro cigarette ads.

known expert Ray Hunt is used, so bronc stompers no longer work in the bronc pens on the Four Sixes. When the geldings are two years old, some are sent to the other 6666 divisions to be taken into remudas there and ridden by cowboys and taught the work of a cow horse. The large red horse barn with its famous 6666 brand emblazoned on the front in white, a familiar picture in Marlboro tobacco advertisements, has been moved from the headquarters of the Four Sixes at Guthrie to the Ranching Heritage Center at Texas Tech University.

Oil discovered on the property in the 1950s has proved enormously beneficial to the ranch and has provided the resources needed to finance the kind of operation it has managed to run. These revenues have allowed the construction of excellent corrals and barns and made possible land acquisitions and development. Perhaps as important as these improvements and expansions, oil has allowed the ranch to be a first-class operation in every way.

Thanks to manager J. J. Gibson, the operations for the roundups these days are well planned and well supplied. Anne Burnett Marion and Gibson continue a long Burnett commitment to having the best ranches, the best horses, the best cattle, and the best cowboys available.

FOUR SIXES RANCH

Green Ranches

Shackelford County near Albany and Texas Panhandle near Vega

Three independent spreads compose the Green ranches run by sons of William Henry Green, a pioneer rancher and livestock trader in West Texas who descended from ancestors who came to the Lone Star State from Tennessee and Missouri. Two brothers named Green were in Texas by the 1830s and saw service in the war against Mexico. It is difficult to be more "Texan" than that. Headquarters for two of the ranches are located in Shackelford County near Albany, and one is at Vega in the Texas Panhandle. Other holdings lie near Breckenridge, Matador, and Dalhart. Unlike many other large ranches in the state whose development was funded by outside money, these ranches resulted from shrewd trading and careful management by a close-knit ranching family that grew up in an area now covered by Hubbard Creek Lake between Albany and Breckenridge.

The story begins around 1885 when young William Henry Green left the family home near present-day Hillsboro in Hill County of Texas in search of his future. Carrying only his meager belongings in a small bag, his bridle, saddle, and blanket, Green stepped off the train in Albany to round up and sell some of the mustangs that his father, Thomas Henry Green, owned with J. J. Witty of Albany and ran on open range in that area. He found the Wittys' dugout headquarters and the herd and liked the country; he decided to stay with the Wittys to work alongside their son, Bert, to learn the ranching business. Green soon spotted an eight-thousand-acre stretch of prime open range running along Hubbard Creek and decided that was the place for him. He sold his father's horse herd but kept back thirty geldings, which he spent one winter along Hubbard Creek breaking by himself, a risky task that shows his confidence and fortitude. In the spring he drove the string of horses to Albany and sold them to Arthur G. Ligertwood of the Matador Ranch for thirty dollars each. The family later learned that one of the horses became a legendary outlaw that was used to test any bronc rider who showed up at the Matador for years to come.

Using the $900.00 from the sale of the horses, Green leased the land along Hubbard Creek from Col. E. S. Graham, prominent early-day land agent for the T. E. and L. Land Company of Louisville, Kentucky, and founder of the city of Graham to the north of the range. Green completed fencing the land easily because individuals holding the property on the various sides of the ranch had already fenced nearly all of it.

Green remained a bachelor for many years and camped alone in a covered wagon beneath some oak trees along Hubbard Creek, where he had his cattle pens and horse corrals. Following a serious illness during one winter, however, Green wisely decided to build a house. Money was scarce in those days, so Green traded a small herd of horses to a man in East Texas for enough one-by-twelve planks to build a structure. Each board was eighteen feet long, so Green cut each one in half and raised a two-room box-and-strip house with walls nine feet high. The family recalls that he "wasted only the sawdust" from the cuts. The two-room house was incorporated into what grew to be a large, rambling ranch house along Hubbard Creek. Green spent his years traveling the ranch country buying and selling horses and cattle and building a herd of cattle.

In 1917 at age fifty, Green married Miss Willie Weaver, then a woman of thirty-four years of age. She was related to the Robertson family, still prominent ranchers in nearby Stephens County near Crystal Falls. She had been reared by the Richey family in that area after being orphaned at an early age. The couple soon had four children: Bill, Tom, Mary Anna, and Bob. Formal education was important to the Greens and still is. Before he left home, the elder Green had earned a bachelor's degree at Trinity University in Tehuacana Hills near Mexia before the school moved to its present location in San Antonio. Miss Weaver took her degree in 1906 at what was then North Texas State Normal School, now the University of North Texas, in Denton and

SCHOOL-CHAPEL

It was known as Squyres' Chapel and stood on the far hill when the teacher in this painting, Miss Willie Weaver, was a small schoolgirl. One day an election was held there and two families who were enemies arrived at the same time. A quarrel ensued and ended in bloodshed. Miss Weaver wrote in her memoirs that concentration on studies was difficult after that day because of the sunlight shining through the bullet holes in the walls. That summer the chapel was dismantled and carted across the valley to its new location and renamed Bethel Chapel, which means "House of God."

Another interesting story involving the history of this building concerns Miss Weaver, the teacher. She wanted to become a schoolteacher, but she was one of many children in her family and funds were short. Mysterioulsy, an envelope with her name on it appeared and in it was enough money to finance her college education. Upon receiving her degree, she returned to teach at Bethel Chapel, where she taught for many years. At age 34 she married Mr. Green who was then 50 years of age. He was someone she had always known and admired, and she suspected him to be her benefactor. Over the years, she asked him many times if he was the one who financed her education. He would never admit it . . . but he never denied it.

GREEN RANCH
"HOME FROM THE HONEYMOON"
AUGUST 1917

THE RANCH HOUSE, AUGUST 1917

Henry and Willie Green have just driven up in their Hupmobile Roadster, the first auto in the county. They are returning from their honeymoon in Denver, Colorado, and are eager to begin their new life together. The ranch house is only a three-room bungalow with no conveniences, save the cistern out back, but over the years Willie Green will make many changes and renovations as her family grows.

The house's original location is now the bottom of Lake Hubbard, and the structure was moved when work began on the dam. Now it stands at the top of the hill with a beautiful view of the lake. The family still gathers there for holidays, parties, and reunions—the children, grandchildren, and great-grandchildren of that happy couple.

taught in schools in the Texas Panhandle and along Hubbard Creek before she married.

The Green children were first instructed at home by their mother and later went to school in Breckenridge and then in Albany. Green bought a house in each of the towns and lived with the family there during the school term. He "commuted" to his ranch work. The family always looked forward to returning to the banks of Hubbard Creek in the summer. All these children would later attend college, primarily New Mexico Military Institute at Roswell. Tom, however, attended Texas Tech University after Green heard an impressive speech at the Bloys Camp Meeting in the Davis Mountains from then-president Clifford B. Jones, the man for whom the athletic stadium at Texas Tech University is named.

Growing up along the creek was practically idyllic for the children. Isolated from the hardly accessible towns of Breckenridge and Albany, the children entertained each other with games, many of which involved horseback riding, always part of their work as well. Bob can recall when he was wrangling horses in the brushy country and had to listen intently in the predawn darkness for the bell the boys had put on the neck of one of the saddle horses before the herd was turned out to graze for the night.

Because of the older than usual age of the parents when they were born, the children all but skipped a generation. Here are second-generation ranchers who live much as others did in the 1940s and 1950s. They also recall names of families as Crudgington, Lawrence, Riley, and Hitson who worked for the ranch. Descendants of these cowhands still live in the area, and many of them still follow the cattle business.

The ranch expanded as time and resources allowed. Green gradually purchased the original 8,000 acres of leased land, mostly in plots of 320 acres, half-sections, as a nester starved out and decided to leave. Green also bought the Roe Ranch adjoining his original land and then purchased,

in 1939, 26,000 acres, part of the Landergin Ranch near Vega in Oldham County in the Texas Panhandle. He also bought the Rockwell Ranch, 17,000 acres along the highway between Abilene and Albany. It is still designated by the name of a former owner, Rockwell and Hill, founders of a chain of lumber outlets. In addition Green leased land where he could find it to graze his herds.

The ranch operated as a family unit until 1950, when Green at age 82 was killed in an automobile accident between Lueders and Avoca as he and Mrs. Green were driving to the Vega Ranch to check on a herd of steers. Mary Anna took the Poindexter Ranch near Ibex where she and her husband, John Mussleman, had been living. Tom took the Vega Ranch, and he traded his two brothers their shares of that ranch for his share of the home ranch along Hubbard Creek. Bill and Bob continued in partnership for several more years until Bill's son, Billy, graduated from Texas Tech University and returned to enter business with his father. Bob's son moved to Dallas, so the two direct descendants of the founder dissolved the partnership. Bill assumed control of a ranch earlier purchased in Hartley and Oldham counties near Dalhart, part of which had been XIT land, and what is called the South Ranch between Albany and Baird. Bill also operates part of the Rockwell as well as the Newell Ranch south of Albany, which he has recently purchased with A. V. Jones, Jr., an Albany oil man. The Poindexter Ranch near Ibex southeast of Albany is still operated by John Mussleman, the widower of Mary Anna Green Mussleman, who died of cancer some years ago. In memory of her, the family hosts an annual benefit called Polo on the Prairie for M. D. Anderson Hospital's cancer research. Bob operates the home ranch and part of the Rockwell as well as the Merrick Davis Ranch, which he leases. The Greens are still expanding their holdings and intend to be in the ranching business for years to come.

The Greens have overcome many problems during their ranching years, but none seemed as threatening as the construction of Hubbard Creek Lake. Water authorities selected the site for a new lake despite the historical significance of the area and the fact that the Green home and headquarters were located in what would become the lake bed. There Green had rounded up his horses, set up his wagon camp, built his rambling home, and raised his four children. The children had memories of playing and working in the bottom lands and on the island in the creek. Despite efforts to stop the project, the Greens eventually accepted payment for the land and gave up their fight. The ranch house was saved by moving it from the lake bed to higher ground, where it stands today. The money paid for the land was invested in more land; included are ten thousand acres formerly owned by the Matador Ranch.

The Greens have diversified their operation. Farming on the irrigated property bordering the lake includes mostly winter wheat for grazing cattle and horses and some hay grazer in the summer. Some acres are devoted to growing coastal Bermuda grass for hay. Some of the Panhandle lands are also used to produce wheat. Brush control methods have run the general gamut of spraying, grubbing, chaining, and burning, but like other ranchers the Greens have not found the magic formula for eradicating the ranges of the parasitic brush. This is one of the reasons Tom moved to the Panhandle—no mesquite and prickly pear.

The Greens are ranchers in the traditional sense. The founder's view of horses differed from that of some older cowmen, such as Dan Waggoner and Burk Burnett, who poured millions of dollars into breeding, showing, and racing quality horse flesh. Green owed his beginning to horses, but he felt they were necessary to, not the priority ingredient of, ranch life. He preferred horses of conformation and disposition fitted to his cattle operation regardless of bloodlines. The Greens are not cattle chasing and roping cowboys, though some of their hands, especially Bob's foreman, Benny Peacock, are excellent cowboys and ropers. Green's sons have followed their father's line of thought, although both have a band of brood mares and quality stallions. Bill has Golden Three Bars out of the famous Hollywood Gold and Doc Bar, and Bob runs Bego Bars, another of the line of Doc Bar blood. Both herds are small, around a dozen mares, but these provide enough geldings to keep the remuda up to the necessary level and to provide replacement mares as well as a few fillies to sell. Bill's son trains and shows cutting horses but still shares his grandfather's views on cow ponies for cattle work.

Cattle have been the major thrust of the Green ranches. At first Longhorns and mixed breeds stocked the ranges as Green traded for what cattle he could find. Later the English breeds, mainly Herefords, ranged in the pastures, and now crossbreeding has taken over as it has in most ranches in the state. Bob developed an interest in Beefmaster cattle about 1975 and has kept heifers and crossbred until his herd is three-fourths Beefmaster. Now he runs Limousin bulls with the cows on the home ranch. On the Merrick Davis Ranch near his Rockwell pasture, he runs Hereford cattle. The herd contains some registered cows he purchased near Watrous, New Mexico; these registered cows are especially large, one of them recently weighing 1,750 pounds when sold. Bill began crossbreeding with Brangus stock and later introduced Charolais and Limousin blood. On the two Albany-area ranches, the Greens calve about three hundred heifers a year, though the number varies with market prices and herd needs.

The founder's philosophy still influences life on the ranch. His conservative ways and positive values have caused the children to develop a fairly simple but comfortable lifestyle. Both Bob and Tom saw service in World War II and traveled much of Europe during that time. Members of the family have cultivated polite friendships and far-reaching social circles including artists, politicians, and such writers as A. C. Greene, perhaps Texas' best-known writer. With their wives, Nancy and Elizabeth, Bob and Bill run a quality livestock operation and conserve wild game, especially deer, by feeding them and not allowing hunting.

Bob, an excellent family and area historian and capable writer and storyteller, has recorded a lot of the stories that he has heard from the region. Many of these were published in the *Albany News*. Bob also served as co-narrator with Marilyn Jacobs of the Fort Griffin Fandangle, an outdoor drama now over fifty years old. Begun by Robert Nail and continued after Nail's death in the late 1960s, the Fandangle has, in Bob's words, "painlessly indoctrinated several generations of youngsters" with the history of the area of the old military fort and town in northern Shackelford County.

Bill has been in every Fandangle performance. He and his son, Billy, have been flag bearers in the figure-eight parade to open the show, and Bill recently portrayed Robert E. Lee, the Confederate military leader, when Lee was still a Union officer stationed at Camp Cooper on the Clear Fork of the Brazos River. Some of the Greens' cowboys also participate in the production of the drama.

Bill recalls many of his father's antics, because as a young man he became Green's driver and drove him and his friends to many stock shows, such as those in Kansas City, Denver, and Fort Worth. One of the humorous stories recalled by the Greens was the time during a severe drought that Jim Nail, the owner of a large ranch to the west of the Greens, found that he was out of water and was forced to sell about five hundred four-year-old cows with their calves, cows that he had held back for a breeding stock when the drought broke. Once the deal was struck, Green took half the herd to his home range and discovered that his entire new herd would probably overstock the range. As luck would have it, rain fell that night over wide areas of the ranch country. By morning Nail discovered that he had caught water in most of his tanks. He called Green to try to back out of the deal. Green, though he decided that he could not handle the extra stock, played his cards wisely and ended up selling the part of the herd still on the Nail ranges back to Nail for a $15.00 a pair profit.

The Greens have managed to put together and continue to expand an impressive ranching operation. Oil revenues have been helpful to them in their efforts and have afforded them the opportunity to construct better pens, make efforts to control brush, and keep the quality of life at a desirable level. Oil is a "bittersweet" blessing to ranching country. The practice of searching and producing damages the land, but, as Bob notes, "every rancher needs a West Texas ranch with oil on it in order to keep up his home ranch and fight the brush." The Greens are energetic and enthusiastic people who have contributed much to life in the Albany area and who display the warm hospitality of ranch culture.

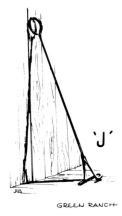

GREEN RANCH

Iron Mountain Ranch

Brewster County near Marathon

Iron Mountain Ranch, located in Brewster County north of the present town of Marathon in the Big Bend area of Texas, was founded in 1881 by Captain Albion Sheppard, who had first come to the area as part of a surveying party when the Southern Pacific Railroad laid its lines through the area. Captain Sheppard donated the land on which the town of Marathon was later built and also suggested that the area reminded him of the plains of Marathon in Greece; hence, he is credited as the source of the exotic name of this town located some sixty miles north of the Rio Grande and near the entrance to the Big Bend National Park. Alpine, a ranching and education center to the west, is the only other town of significant size in Brewster County. The ranch is bounded on the south by U.S. Highway 90 and on the east by U.S. Highway 385 from Fort Stockton. On the north and west sides the ranch extends into rugged mountains.

Geographic landmarks enclosed within boundaries of the 45,000-acre ranch include part of the Glass Mountains, known for shiny particles in the stone that glisten in the sun. Leonard Mountain also stands on the ranch. The most dominating feature, however, is Iron Mountain, a 30-to-50-million-year-old intrusive formation that stands about a thousand feet in height, is a mile long, and runs about one-half mile in width at its widest point.

Over the years the ranch and its surrounding area have proved to be a rich natural site. Staff members from the Smithsonian Institution have collected fossils there and on the neighboring Hess Ranch for over three decades and deposited them in its exhibits. The Capitan Reef is exposed in Gilliland Canyon, which runs through the ranch. This is the same geologic feature that is exposed on the El Capitan Mountain located many miles to the north in the Guadalupe Mountains National Park east of El Paso.

Originally, the ranch ranged up to 27,000 head of sheep shipped in by rail from California by Captain Sheppard. Although sheep grazing continued for many years, during at least the last half-century cattle have been the only domesticated animals grazed on the ranch. The early bloodlines were Herefords. These were later crossed with Angus and then with Brangus. In this section of the state grazing will usually permit one animal unit per each fifty acres, a far cry from that available on the lush pasture lands in the better-watered areas of the state.

Some early fencing of the ranch with stacked rock walls is still evident. William B. Blakemore II, current owner of the ranch, indicates that these walls are still in remarkably good condition, and he notes that evidently over a long period of time considerable effort went into the construction of these walls and some rock corrals. The exterior fencing of the ranch is typically three to four strands of barbed wire with some drift fences used in the mountainous sections. Some net wire fencing stretches across the flat lands.

Ownership of the ranch has extended through several families since Captain Sheppard sold the ranch in 1887. In early years the Wardlaw family from Del Rio leased the land and then operated it as a sheep ranch in the 1930s. Still later, a partnership called Skinner and Bynum lent its name to Iron Mountain Ranch. The J. M. West family purchased and operated the ranch for a time as a division of the Longfellow Ranch, located about forty miles down Highway 90 from the Iron Mountain Ranch. The Longfellow Ranch consisted of about 220,000 acres and was run by the West-Pyle Cattle Company. Principal owners were J. M. West, Sr., and T. M. Pyle. Buck Pyle, son of T. M., continued to work for the West family for many years after the West-Pyle partnership was dissolved. Later operators included J. M. West, Jr., and Wesley West, sons of J. M. West, Sr. Later the ranch was inherited by J. M. West, Jr.'s daughter Marian West, then the wife of William B. Blakemore II, who still controls the ranch.

Buildings found on the ranch are representative of the area. Remains of a one-and-a-half-story stone house stand near the south end of Iron Mountain. There is no reason to doubt that this is a dwelling erected by Captain Sheppard during the time that he controlled the ranch. It is built of local stone, with limited use of cement and considerable use of local clays. Near the ruins of this structure is an old adobe wall, thought to be remains of a barn erected on the site.

The current headquarters has two stone houses, one small one and another larger one with heavy walls of gray granite quarried on the ranch. It was probably built in the late 1920s or early 1930s by S. P. Skinner when he controlled the property. The house has been remodeled and serves as a guesthouse as well as housing for hunters on the ranch. Other barns and outbuildings are located at the ranch headquarters.

Game abounds on the ranch, but the hunting is not leased except for some commercial hunting of aoudad sheep, an imported Barbary sheep from Africa. These have multiplied in the region since Cap Yates, who at one time owned part of the Iron Mountain Ranch, imported them. Some years ago, however, after many years of fairly static population, the number of aoudads exploded and now between three and four thousand head of these animals roam the Glass Mountains area. Mr. Blakemore has recently counted over five hundred of these Barbary sheep in one herd. He said the sight reminded him of an African migration. Other game animals on the ranch include elk and white-tailed deer from the Carmen Mountains of Old Mexico, as well as mule deer. Although crossbreeding between mule and white-tailed deer was earlier thought to be impossible, there is scientific evidence of some hybridization between this kind of white-tailed deer and the mule deer. Other game animals include antelope, javelina, and blue quail. Transplanted wild turkeys have been located on the ranch, and porcupines are sometimes seen. A protected species found on the ranch is Mearns' quail, also known as fools' quail or crazy quail, because of their shy, gentle nature.

Predators found in the region include coyotes, which prey especially on the antelope young, as well as numerous mountain lions. The latter species has really made a significant recovery from a state where they were thought to be almost extinct. Frequent evidence of their kills is found in the region.

The current cattle operation is a cow-calf operation run by foreman Lloyd Stuessy. At one time he kept from four to five Mexican cowboys on the ranch, but since labor laws have made this no longer feasible, Mr. Stuessy runs the ranch largely by himself and hires day workers to help with the working of the cattle. Branding is accomplished by a combination of roping and dragging and using working tables in the substantial pens and chutes found on the ranch. The brand is 111, called the One-Eleven brand, which Mr. Blakemore selected after J. M. West, Jr.'s death. Mr. West had liked those numbers, had even used them as his police call sign, and Mr. Blakemore felt that this was an appropriate step to take. Earlier the brand had been the B Bar of the West-Pyle Cattle Company.

Extensive breeding of Quarter Horses has been carried on on the ranch in years past, though with the current market situation, this operation has been scaled down. Bloodlines include those from the King Ranch, especially Peppy bloodlines, and some use of Waggoner Ranch bloodlines. In the early 1980s more than a hundred broodmares roamed the ranch. Some of these were bred to some topflight stallions belonging to the Super Syndicate, an investment group that is now dissolved. Most of these stallions were descendants of Doc bloodlines, and stallions included Doc Kiote and Doc Elena.

No minerals, either oil or such hard minerals as precious metals or mercury, are known to exist in commercial quan-

OLD HOMESTEAD

All that remains today of the original homestead are portions of the house walls with a few wooden beams and a few yards away the adobe wall of what was once the barn and corral. These dwellings were probably erected by Captain Sheppard, the founder of the ranch, in 1881. He chose well the location of the buildings on the south side of Iron Mountain, for it was well protected from the cold north winds and had a small running brook just in front.

Today's headquarters is located on the east side of the mountain. The newer family hacienda built by William B. Blakemore II is equally picturesque. It is located on the far side of the mountain shown in the left background of the painting. The house stands at six thousand feet with the panorama of Gilliland Canyon far below.

tities on the ranch. Some dry holes for oil wells were drilled in the wildcat days of the 1920s but produced no favorable results.

With cross fencing today, pastures on the ranch usually range around five thousand acres or less. There are some smaller pastures and some traps, or small fenced areas where cattle can be held. Livestock productivity depends upon the availability of water, and numerous good water wells are found on the ranch. Water is pumped into holding tanks by windmills and electric pumps. Some dirt tanks have been scooped out in the soil but are good mainly in the rainy season. Any digging of deep tanks would descend to the level of gravel and stone, and these efforts have proved impractical.

On the ranch, cowboy rather than vaquero gear is found. Little or no use of tapaderos is necessary since the brush is not a major factor in working the cattle. Saddles will typically have swelled forks and rolled cantles, and the rest of the gear—hats, spurs, ropes—is of the sort associated with the cowboy.

Flora on the ranch is fully discussed in an excellent volume by Barton H. Warnock. It includes sotol or maguey, a cactuslike plant that raises a tall shoot and has white flowers. This flourishes in the foothills. Also found are short mesquite, soapberry, white brush, huisache, catclaw, and juniper or cedar. A wide spectrum of grama grasses includes sideoats, blue, and black, as well as King Ranch bluestem and others. Tabosa grass is found in some of the flats. Vine mesquites and sacahuista, or bear grass, are found on some parts of the ranch as are buffalo and sacaton grasses.

A wide variety of cacti can be found, including cholla and some prickly pear, but this growth is small and scattered and does not pose a range management problem in this region, a sharp contrast to ranches in North Texas and South Texas as well as other parts of West Texas. Little efforts of brush control have been necessary but when necessary have been directed mostly at spot-grubbing juniper as well as white brush in the draws.

It is believed that there must have been small basins that caught and held water during the rainy season and attracted Indians, probably in the times of prehistory. Many signs of Indian habitation have been found on the ranch, especially in the form of burn circles and rubbings on large stones. The burn circles were probably where the Indians cooked the sotol cabbages, the succulent growth found at the base of the sotol plant. The rubbings are polished tops of boulders, which Warnock believes were left that way by Indians who long ago used the stone surfaces to remove the oil and hair from hides during the tanning process. Also found are grinding or mortar holes, circular indentations one to two feet in depth in the stone. These were used by Indians to grind grain and seeds. The great Comanche war trail passes by the ranch and splits north of the Glass Mountains, with one branch going through Fort Stockton and the other coming around on the eastern side of the Glass Mountains.

The Blakemore family, in whose name the ranch has operated for the last few decades, is indeed an interesting one. William B. Blakemore II is a veteran of the Air Corps during World War II and also saw service in the Air Force during the Korean War. He manages a complex set of companies called Alpha 21, or the Alpha Group, a family-owned corporation responsible for oil, ranch, real estate, and investment activities, and currently is also interested in bioremediation activities and environmental concerns related to the oil business. Blakemore is the longest-serving commissioner on the Texas Department of Public Safety Board, where he twice served as chairman during his fourteen years of service. An annual meeting of Company E of the Texas Rangers is held on the ranch. He currently is serving his fourth term on an advisory panel to the U.S. Army for

34

officer accession for the active army and reserve forces. He has found his dozen or so years in that capacity to be very rewarding.

Blakemore and his first wife, Marian West Blakemore, had five children: James Marion, William Blanton, Jr., Bruce Allen, Margene, and Virginia. Following the untimely death of his first wife, Blakemore married Emily Elizabeth Blakemore, a recent widow who had two children, Herbert and Emily, who are presently students at Vanderbilt University.

The Iron Mountain Ranch indeed has a colorful history. One of the more interesting events that happened on the ranch involves the famous story of the brindle bull yearling branded MURDER. The event occurred in January of 1890, when Henry Harrison Powe, a rancher in the area, had a confrontation with Fine Gilliland, another area rancher, over the ownership of a brindle bull calf that showed up in a herd being gathered on the Iron Mountain Ranch. The bitter conflict that emerged between the two resulted in a gun fight between Powe and Gilliland in which Powe was fatally shot. The bull over which the argument had ensued was later branded with its famous brand, and, so the story goes, the animal was later included in a trail herd driven to Montana.

There seems every reason to believe that the incident is factually reported, and it is indeed one of the famous stories associated with this historic region of the country. Gilliland's role in the fight gave his name to the canyon that runs through the ranch.

This ranch represents part of the colorful and rich history of grazing in Texas. Its diversity in flora and fauna as well as its geologic features, history, and lore mark it as a valuable part of our culture.

IRON MOUNTAIN RANCH

King Ranch

South Texas between Corpus Christi and Brownsville

The principal ranges of the King Ranch, one of the truly historic ranches in the world, stretch along the Gulf Coast of Texas, where at one time it occupied more than a million and a quarter acres that cover parts of eight present-day counties. The original piece of property, known as the Santa Gertrudis, was held first under a grant from the King of Spain by José Domingo de la Garza, and then by José Pérez Rey. The latter's heirs sold it to Captain Richard King.

This Richard King, the founder, was a unique man. Born on July 10, 1824, in New York, he came to the region following varied experiences in the river boat trade in the South, experience that provided his basic education. He came to the Rio Grande area during the time of the war with Mexico in 1847 as a pilot for Captain Mifflin Kenedy, a man slightly older than King but a kindred spirit. The two became partners in a river boat company known as Kenedy and Company. After the flurry of transporting men and supplies up the Rio Grande for the invasion of Mexico, and back down again after the conflict had ended, King decided to go into ranching to offset the lack of traffic on the river. One of the significant influences on him was Robert E. Lee, then assigned to the Department of Texas by the U.S. Army. Lee convinced King that this part of Texas, known as the Wild Horse Desert, had enormous potential as cattle country.

In 1853 the determined King located a ranch headquarters on a 75,000-acre tract along the only source of fresh water in the area, Santa Gertrudis Creek, in the dangerous Nueces Strip, a hotly contested piece of real estate between the Rio Grande, which the Texans had claimed as the border with Mexico, and the Nueces River, which Mexico had insisted was the border. The region became a virtual no man's land for many years, and no man or his livestock was safe from depredation from numerous outlaws and rustlers who found the lawlessness of the strip to their liking. King and his men held their fledgling kingdom by force of arms and fought numerous skirmishes with Mexican banditos.

In 1854 King married Henrietta Chamberlain, the daughter of a Presbyterian minister serving as a missionary in Brownsville. He had met her during his river boat days. She became the first lady and cultural leader in this isolated vastness. From this union came the influence and individuals who were to create and carry on one of the greatest ranches in the world.

King first supplemented wild stock on the ranch with additional Longhorn cattle and mustang horses bought cheaply in Mexico. He tried several brands for cattle but settled on the now-famous Running W. Being in the part of Texas close to Mexico, it is natural that the men working cattle on the ranch would be Mexican vaqueros, not Anglo cowboys. The knowledge and techniques of working cattle in Mexico preceded by many decades the development in Texas. The original vaqueros whom King brought to the ranch have proven to be ideally suited for the country and the work. Even today the names and bloodlines of some of the original vaqueros are still represented there: Cavazos, Mendietta, Maldonado, Quintanilla, Treviño, Montalvo, Silva, Rodríquez, and Cortinas, to name some of the most prominent. It has been said that the ranch hires only 10 percent of its help and raises the other 90 percent.

King was a far-sighted cattleman and saw early in his career that fencing was necessary to upgrade his breeding stock. Since barbed wire was unavailable at this time, he traded cattle for lumber and began fencing huge tracts. Today, if strung in one direction, fences on the ranch, made of a specially designed net wire, would reach from the ranch to Boston. In addition, he brought in shorthorn cattle from Kentucky. Capital from this enterprise came from a new boost in the river boat traffic to overcome the Civil War blockade of the South. The boats that he and Kenedy still held in partnership were hauling expensive cotton down the river to British ships waiting for the precious cargo at Brazos Santiago.

By the end of the Civil War, the ranch consisted of more than 300,000 acres, made up of the original Santa Gertrudis grant, Laureles, and Agua Dulce. In 1860 Kenedy had bought a half-interest in the expanded enterprise, but in

ALTA DE BURRO, SANTA GERTRUDIS DIVISION

This is the site of the last wooden windmill on the King Ranch. The use of windmills saved the ranch in the late 1800s as did oil many years later. The cattle are Santa Gertrudis developed on the King Ranch and were the first American breed of cattle to be registered. Note the unique method of securing wire fencing to posts (at far right of the painting).

Although the windmill no longer stands in its original location, it has been preserved and is now located close to the main house in the backyard of Tio Kleberg.

1868 the partnership broke up and Kenedy took control of the Laureles section, which Mrs. King later bought and returned to the ranch. King continued to add to his holdings—the San Juan Carricitos and other lands were purchased during King's lifetime. Major divisions came to include Encino and Norias. Financing for this expansion came from Francisco Yturria of Brownsville and Swante Magnus Swenson, then a New York financier but later founder of extensive ranches in North Texas. Both families are described in this volume.

The problems that had plagued early Texas ranchers affected King as well. The major problem was that there were no available markets for beef. King competed in the hide and tallow market by building a rendering plant on Santa Gertrudis Creek a few miles north of the present location of the ranch headquarters. A historical marker on Texas Highway 141 denotes the location. After the Civil War, King soon sent his cattle up the trail to the railheads in Kansas. In fact, King envisioned a fenced "highway" that would take cattle from Texas to Canada. The introduction of barbed wire about this time provided the means he felt were necessary to bring the project to realization, but he was unable to do so. Other problems to be solved included a lack of reliable water sources, improved beef cattle with resistance to the heat and parasites of the region, tick fever, poor quality grass, and insidiously spreading brush and cactus.

Following the death of King in 1885, Robert Kleberg, Sr., the family lawyer who later married King's youngest daughter, Alice, was asked by Mrs. King to assume managerial responsibilities of the ranch in a time of crisis for the cattle industry because of drought, disastrous markets, and uncertainty over the future of ranching. The contributions of members of the Kleberg family are many. Robert, Sr., continued to add to the holdings of the ranch. Following the discovery that a tick caused the fever that plagued imported cattle lacking natural immunities to the disease, he built dipping vats to help eliminate the menace. In addition, under Kleberg's direction, the ranch was instrumental in

founding the city of Kingsville on land donated for the city site. He helped build two railroads and supported the dredging project to make Corpus Christi a deep-sea port. By the time of Mrs. King's death in 1925, the ranch consisted of a million acres, and by the death of Kleberg in 1932, in the throes of the Great Depression, the ranch had grown to 1.25 million acres. Including ranches on foreign soil in Latin America, Morocco, and Australia, it would eventually rise to 13 million acres. But Kleberg solved another critical problem before his death. Drillers discovered artesian water below the five-hundred-foot depth, and eventually over three hundred wells dotted the ranch to provide water for cattle in remote sections away from the creek and unreliable tanks scooped out of the ground. This discovery also allowed people to move into that region to develop it.

Following the death of the elder Kleberg, Robert Kleberg, Jr. (Bob), and his brother, Richard (Dick), took over. Bob ran the ranch on a daily basis; Dick became a legislator and handled ranch business. They continued in the vein of Captain King and their father by expanding the ranch and by perfecting the breed of cattle for which the ranch has become known, the deep red Santa Gertrudis. In addition, Bob added a thousand miles of wire fencing. These three Klebergs have been important to the management of the ranch, but so have others. Robert, Sr.'s nephew, Caesar Kleberg, for example, ran the Norias division for many years before his death in 1946. Other names appear in this prestigious list— Sam Chesshire, who succeeded Caesar at Norias, was a former Texas Ranger as was Charley Burwell, who ran the Laureles. Jim McBride, who ran the Encino division, and Belton K. Johnson, Robert Kleberg, Jr.'s nephew, are also part of this line of management in this generation. Leonard Stiles recently retired as manager of the Santa Gertrudis after many years of service and still lives on the ranch. Management from 1974 to 1988 included Dick Kleberg, Jr., businessman James H. Clement, stockman John B. Armstrong, Tio Kleberg, and W. B. Yarborough, all direct descendants of King or Kleberg or in-laws. Roger L. Jarvis, who followed

Darwin E. Smith, now serves as president and chief executive officer of the ranch and will lead it into the future.

The ranch is still almost a principality unto itself. Five hundred people live on the Santa Gertrudis division alone. Children of ranch employees attend their own school from kindergarten through eighth grade, with a total of around eighty students. Their high school education is completed in Kingsville. The famous Santa Gertrudis mansion sits on a hilltop at the headquarters. The twenty-five room house, which can sleep fifty-four people, was completed in 1915, after the previous large frame headquarters building burned in 1912. The mission motif throughout the house is intended to remind descendants of Mrs. King's background as the daughter of a Presbyterian missionary. The battlements on the roof line and tower give a view of the plain for miles around, once an essential advantage in the days when surprise attacks of banditos were not unknown. The large stained-glass windows crafted by Tiffany's of New York, a firm that also furnished the home, have recently been completely restored. Nearby stand numerous other buildings, including the commissary in which Richard King's office was once located, stables, and numerous other structures. A large garage designed to hold automobiles has been converted into a pool house. Formal dinner is served in the evening for family members and special guests, with distinctive china and silver, by waiters in white coats. The customary pattern is for the guests to meet in the library at 7:00 and for dinner to be served at 7:30. Coats and ties are expected for men, a practice begun by Mrs. King and continued by her daughter Alice Kleberg to remind everyone that polite culture still exists in this remote area.

In *Cattle Kings of Texas*, C. L. Douglas notes that in the 1930s the ranch had 125,000 head of cattle made up of "fifty thousand cows, as many steers, nearly half as many calves, and three thousand bulls of the Brahma, Shorthorn, Hereford, and Santa Gertrudis breeds" along with 2,500 head of horses (p. 81). Some years income from the sale of horses exceeded that from the cattle. Usually 60,000 head of choice cattle stock the ranch along with a 400 head of some of the best Quarter Horses in the world. Over the years income from the ranch has been supplemented by a long productive relationship with Humble Oil and Refining Company, now Exxon Corporation; later the ranch formed its own energy corporation headquartered in Houston, Texas.

Among the contributions of this ranching heritage is the development of the Santa Gertrudis cattle. Over thirty years of development and crossbreeding Shorthorns and Brahmas were consumed before the breed was firmly set. The best-known sire in the line was a bull named simply Monkey, an animal considered the epitome of the Santa Gertrudis breed. Now, through scientific breeding methods, the ranch still strives to improve productivity of its cattle and closely monitors its success in doing so. These cattle have been raised in various areas where the British breeds do not do well because of parasites and hot, humid conditions, including Cuba, Panama, Guatemala, Mexico, Colombia, Venezuela, Peru, the Virgin Islands, the Philippines, and even Australia. In addition, the ranch crossbreeds with Gelbvieh, a German breed, and Red Angus. The ranch has repaid the world for the Longhorn stock with which the ranch began by providing a uniquely adapted breed of cattle for the area in which they were developed.

A famous line of Quarter Horses has been a credit to the ranch. The most famous is Old Sorrel, whose bloodline has been significant to Quarter Horse history. Caesar Kleberg bought the horse as a colt from George Clegg of nearby Alice, a town named for the wife of Robert Kleberg, Sr. Later, Old Sorrel was bred to fifty high-quality English Thoroughbred racing mares. Inbreeding and line breeding with Old Sorrel's blood established the dominant strain of King Ranch Quarter Horses. One of the most famous animals from this line was Wimpy, the first horse entered in the register of the American Quarter Horse Association. A statue of him stands in front of the association's office in Amarillo. Other famous stallions include Bill Cody, Tired Hand, Peppy, Babe Mac C, Rey del Rancho, Hot Shot, and

MRS. KING'S HACIENDA

The frame house "ghosted" through the painting was built for her by her husband, Captain Richard King, and greatly expanded over the years to accommodate the family and guests. It burned to the ground during the night in 1912—all occupants were safe. Mrs. King asked her son-in-law, Robert Kleberg, Sr., to build, on the same spot, a fireproof home that would be elegant yet very comfortable, where the men could walk in wearing their boots. The result is this magnificent twenty-five-room home with a central courtyard that has hosted the rich, famous, and not so famous for seventy-six years.

DIPPING VATS

During the last two decades of the nineteenth century the U.S. cattle industry was well on its way to being destroyed by an insignificant little bug—a tick. Efforts to eradicate the tick were centered on the King Ranch in 1894 when Robert Kleberg, Sr., built the first dipping vat, filled it with oil and sulphur, and plunged his cattle in over their heads. Although Longhorns were immune to the fever caused by the ticks, they carried the tick and spread it to the Shorthorns and Herefords, so all were dipped. The original vat, seen in this painting at far right under the shed, is still intact.

Little Man. The two most productive Quarter Horse stallions on the ranch are Mr. San Peppy and Peppy San Badger. Dr. John Toelkes oversees the horse breeding program, and Joe Stiles sees to the breaking and training. The quality of these horses makes them such valuable assets that the ranch cannot afford to sell them, though there is an annual sale of some King Ranch horses. Buster Welch, a renowned cutting horse trainer, has trained many of the ranch's cutting horses at his facility near Trent, west of Abilene, and has won several national titles on King Ranch horses.

The Thoroughbred racing stables were established in 1934 by Robert Kleberg, Jr. Success for the distinctive brown-and-white silks of the ranch came in 1946 when Assault, perhaps the most famous of King Ranch Thoroughbreds, won the triple crown of racing—Preakness, Belmont, and Kentucky Derby—and in 1950 when Middleground, a half-brother, won the Kentucky Derby and Belmont. Both were sons of Bold Venture, a Derby winner purchased by the Klebergs as a sire. Other famous names include Cryptic, Rejected, Better Self, To Market, Free America, and Mamboretti. After Bob Kleberg's death in 1974, the Thoroughbred operation was relocated to Lexington, Kentucky, known as the home of Thoroughbred racing stock. The stud barn at the ranch with its rubber matting to prevent slipping by the horses is occupied by Quarter Horse stallions.

If, as some say, cattle are just individual factories for turning grass into beef, then it stands to reason that the better the rangeland, the better producers of beef the cattle are. The ranch has led in the development of techniques to control the brush, using bulldozers and developing root plowing techniques. To overcome nutrient deficiencies in native grasses found on the ranch, personnel, led by agronomist Nico Diaz, developed such grasses as King Ranch bluestem and Kleberg bluestem to provide nutritious forage well suited to the climate. The problems detected by King have one by one been solved by his descendants. In addition, the ranch has 63,000 acres of farming of milo maize and cotton.

Considerable effort has gone into hunting and game conservation, including predator control, especially with coyotes, since they are a particularly strong threat to quail population. Numerous mountain lions have been spotted on the ranch over the years. Cars outfitted for hunting deer, quail, and antelope came to be associated with the ranch, and two of these are in the ranch family museum in Kingsville.

Because of widespread public interest, the ranch has special outlets for the public. The King Ranch Saddle Shop, an outgrowth of the original saddlery that made gear uniquely suited for work on the ranch, also produces goods for sale to the public in the form of leather purses and other fine goods. It has the only saddle shop found in Kingsville, still a headquarters of ranching culture in this largely agricultural region. Guided tours of the ranch are available. Memorabilia in the form of photographs, saddles, and vehicles are found in the Henrietta Memorial Center in downtown Kingsville, located in a spacious abandoned but refurbished ice house that the King Ranch once used to manufacture ice for railroad shipping from the Rio Grande Valley and for local residents. It is named for Henrietta Rosa Kleberg Larkin Armstrong, one of the famous daughters of the family.

The reputation and romantic aura of the King Ranch place it in a category of the most famous. Even though the vast reaches of the interior of the ranch, now 825,000 acres (its foreign holdings mostly dissolved), are seen by only a few eyes outside those who work for the ranch, the romantic image of this story is immense. Because of the wealth and far-reaching influence of the ranch and its personnel, the mention of King Ranch triggers a response in virtually anyone even vaguely familiar with ranching anywhere in the world.

KING RANCH

Lambshead Ranch (J. A. Matthews)

Shackelford-Throckmorton Counties North of Albany

Named for an early settler of the region, Thomas Lambshead, of Devon, England, Lambshead Ranch lies north of the town of Albany in northern Shackelford and southern Throckmorton counties. Founded by J. A. Matthews in the 1870s, the ranch now includes some forty thousand acres of rolling land composed of limestone uplands and river bottom with several miles of the Clear Fork of the Brazos River watering its acres. Near the ranch are the ruins of Fort Griffin, the post–Civil War military post, and the site of the town commonly known as Griffin or Griffin Flat. Just across the river north of the ranch is a granite marker indicating the site of Camp Cooper, where Col. Robert E. Lee commanded a contingent of cavalry in those tense days before the Civil War. Here he toughened for the severe tests ahead and gained field experience pursuing Indians across the sun-bleached plains. In correspondence back to Virginia he referred to his Texas home as a "desert of dullness." The route of the Butterfield Stage Line, a link from St. Louis to San Francisco in the 1850s, crossed the ranch, and two marble markers indicate known points on the road.

The Matthews and Reynolds families, joined through marriage of several of their children, came to the area in the late 1850s and by the 1860s were in the cattle business, largely by branding Longhorn stock that had grown up wild along the Clear Fork. Comanche Indians still raided in the area, and the settlers had more than one brush with them. During the later stages of the Civil War, when the frontier had little or no organized protection from the Indians, the Reynolds family joined others in the area who "forted up" for mutual protection at nearby Fort Davis in what is now Stephens County in a cluster of picket houses. The Matthews family sought protection at Fort Owl Head in present-day Shackelford County. In one skirmish with the Comanches, George Reynolds was wounded in the abdomen by an arrow, the point of which remained in his body for years. Later, in St. Louis, accompanied by the famous trail driver Shanghai Pierce, Reynolds had the point ex-

tracted by a surgeon named Lewis. The steel point, the silver-mounted bridle of the horse ridden by the Indian who shot Reynolds, and the pistol with which Si Hough, a companion, shot the Indian are today on display in the National Cowboy Hall of Fame in Oklahoma City.

J. A. Matthews married Sallie Reynolds on Christmas Day in 1876 in the Reynolds house in Reynolds Bend of the Clear Fork. The restored house is on property controlled by the ranch today. An account of her experiences on the frontier is found in her classic volume *Interwoven: A Pioneer Chronicle*, now considered one of the best of its kind. Found here are incidents that record the finest efforts of settlers to cope with the demands of the frontier existence and not only survive but also thrive. The spirit of these people is well represented by the account of this unique frontier lady. The Reynolds men, brothers of Mrs. Matthews, drove herds of Longhorn cattle over vast portions of the West and established ranches wherever they went. Among them are the Long X Ranch and Davis Mountain Ranch near Kent in far West Texas, the George Reynolds Ranch at Pecos City, the Glenn Reynolds Ranch near Globe, Arizona, the Park Springs Ranch in New Mexico, and other ranches in Colorado, Arizona, and Wyoming.

Incidents resulting from this travel are the stuff of legend. For example, a herd of Matthews-Reynolds cattle gathered along the Clear Fork was bought by Charles Goodnight to help stock his JA Ranch in Palo Duro Canyon. Legend has it that several buffalo calves in the herd provided some of the breeding stock for the herd of buffalo that Goodnight kept on the ranch in later years, some of which served as the mascots for West Texas State University in Canyon. W. D. Reynolds accompanied the body of famous trail driver Oliver Loving back to Weatherford, Texas, from Fort Sumner, New Mexico, for burial after Loving died of blood poisioning from an arrow wound. Pulitzer Prize–winning novelist Larry McMurtry apparently borrowed from this incident in his widely acclaimed *Lonesome Dove*. Glenn

CHRISTMAS DAY 1876
LAMBSHEAD RANCH

SALVANT

REYNOLDS HOME

This was a very special Christmas Day celebration in 1876, for that day J. A. Matthews and Sallie Reynolds were united in marriage. The wedding took place next to the Christmas tree in the front rooms of her parents' home. The guests arrived and so did the wedding cake to be set on the table in the kitchen beside the punch bowl. After the ceremony and congratulations, the happy couple left in their new buggy, a gift from the bride's oldest brother. It snowed the day before but that simply didn't dampen any spirits on that happy day.

The bride and groom are the parents of 94-year-old Watt Matthews, who still runs the Lambshead Ranch. These Texas ranchers are made of sturdy stock.

THE DUGOUT

When winter approaches and the cattle need to be cared for, cowboys are sent out, usually by two's, to each of the far sections of the ranch. This section has a dugout that will be home for the cowboys for the season. With three-foot-thick walls on three sides and the good warm earth on the north side, the fireplace will keep the place warm all winter.

Watt Matthews, whose family began this ranch, is a great believer in the preservation of his family's heritage and has undertaken to restore all of the family homes and structures on his ranch. What a wonderful legacy for generations to come.

Reynolds' efforts to establish a ranch in Arizona resulted in his untimely death at the hands of an outlaw Apache whom Reynolds, at that time serving as sheriff, was transporting to prison. This family provided several frontiersmen of the sort that promoted the romance often associated with that era.

The work of J. A. Matthews in establishing this and other ranches is indeed a remarkable saga. At one time Matthews controlled hundreds of thousands of acres in northern Shackelford County. He did not own many of those acres because at that time ownership of the range was not a common practice. Once that pattern of ownership appeared clearly to him, however, he began to buy and homestead property until he had accumulated a considerable stretch of West Texas ranch land. Since he controlled the property but did not have sufficient operating capital, Matthews took in several partners under the MO brand and operated the ranch under that name. Five years later the partnership was dissolved and the cattle were split among the various members of the partnership. Ranches that resulted were the T. G. Hendrick, the X Ranch at Reynolds Round Mountain Headquarters, the Merrick Davis Ranch, and the Bill Davis Ranch along Paint Creek. As his part Matthews took possession of the acreage that still makes up the bulk of the property known today as Lambshead Ranch. He registered the AV brand, still used today for the ranch, in 1885.

Hereford cattle were introduced into the area that same year. Although for many years the ranch used Durhams as well as other breeds, the breed of choice eventually became Hereford because, when the cattle were forced to fend for themselves on the parched range during one of the major droughts that occasionally plagued the area, the Herefords proved their thriftiness by surviving in the greatest numbers when the rains finally came. Although some crossbreeding with Angus has been tried on the ranch

lately, Lambshead Ranch remains committed to the Hereford breed.

The ranch has raised only utility horses for working cattle, not for showing or racing. At first, the ranch kept a Welsh stallion and some Spanish brood mares. Later, for a brief time, an Arabian stallion served as herd sire. A small herd of brood mares is now kept on the ranch and has as its stallion the Quarter Horse named Go Dog Go. The herd ranges in the neighborhood of twenty-five, a number that includes some mules used to pull wagons.

The contribution of the family to the community has been substantial. They have been instrumental in founding the local bank, the Presbyterian church, and a now-defunct private school and college. J. A. Matthews himself served as a judge of Shackelford County and was also a leader in the eradication of fever ticks in the area by allowing the dipping vats on Lambshead Ranch to serve a large number of area ranchers for the regular dipping required by law.

In the 1940s management of the ranch passed to Watkins Reynolds Matthews, the youngest of nine children born to J. A. and Sallie Matthews. Watt, as he is widely known, has become one of the best known and most widely honored ranchers in the state. Now well into his nineties, he is only the second manager the ranch has had, certainly a record for longevity. He still brands each calf on the ranch, though he admits he is cautious around cattle since he is not as agile as he once was. A Princeton University graduate of 1921, Watt has been honored by the state of Texas and other organizations for his work in historical preservation. He has been on the board of and honored by such organizations as the Texas Hereford Association, the American Hereford Association, the National Cowboy Hall of Fame, and many others. He has been host to the late President Lyndon B. Johnson and his wife, Lady Bird, Governor John Connally, and many other notable personalities of the day. He was the subject of a PBS program, *Home—Where the Heart Is*, with

Lady Bird Johnson and former San Antonio mayor Henry Cisneros. Watt is a kind and generous man, and his hospitality at Lambshead Ranch has become legendary.

Watt's work in preserving historic buildings on the ranch is among his most notable contributions. These include the Reynolds House, in which his parents were married, and the Stone Ranch house and outbuildings, where his mother lived briefly as a child. The house is thought to have been constructed by Capt. Newton C. Givens of the U.S. Second Dragoons in 1858. At that time, it was the western-most Anglo habitation between Fort Worth and the New Mexico settlements. Watt has also restored a stone dugout and the house of his uncle, Nathan Bartholomew, in Reynolds Bend, and built a replica of the schoolhouse that his father and others constructed in Reynolds Bend. In this beautiful spot along the river Watt hosts the annual Sampler of the Fort Griffin Fandangle, an outdoor historical drama depicting the settlement of the area. He has been a longtime supporter of the Fandangle Association and, for several years, the president of the Board of Directors. He provides mules to pull the replica of the Butterfield Stage Coach and stores the rolling stock on the ranch. He is also active in the Old Jail Art Foundation in Albany.

In addition to his work in restoring buildings, Watt has led by example in wildlife conservation. He has managed the quail, turkey, and deer population on the ranch by selective harvesting and feeding until these game species flourish. For many years he encouraged the trapping of wild turkeys by game biologists to be transplanted to other areas. He also manages the herds of feral hogs on the ranch and annually slaughters several for use in the ranch's kitchen and shares the meat with friends and neighbors. He maintains a small herd of Longhorn cattle, which he brands with the gourd brand long associated with the ranch. As a reminder of the massive herds of shaggy brown bison that once crowded to the Clear Fork in the hot summers, Watt keeps a small herd of buffalo on the ranch. When the herd exceeds twenty in number, the surplus animals are slaughtered for meat to be used on the ranch, and the hides are tanned for decorative purposes.

His work in range conservation by grubbing mesquite and prickly pear and controlled burning has been a model of such practices. But he has maintained the traditional look of the ranch by camouflaging the steel cattle guards with cedar posts and being cautious with brush clearing. So successful has he been in maintaining a traditional look that some of the television film and still shots advertising Marlboro cigarettes have been shot for several years on the ranch.

At the headquarters is the cook shack where meals are prepared daily for the cowboys and guests; the original ranch house, expanded to include modern conveniences; and several other houses for family members who visit the ranch often. Also there is the bunkhouse in which Watt, a bachelor, still sleeps. In a picket house made of upright crossties and chinked with mortar is a fine library of Texana and Western Americana that includes such writers as Elmer Kelton, A. C. Greene, Curry Holden, Tom Lea, J. Evetts Haley, John Graves, T. R. Fehrenbach, J. Frank Dobie, Charles Siringo, Rupert N. Richardson, Carl Coke Rister, Edgar Rye, Conrad Richter, and John Erickson alongside books on Frederic Remington and Charles A. Russell. The focus of Watt's interest is apparent in his library.

Methods of working the cattle on the ranch have become mechanized. The use of squeeze chutes and working tables has replaced roping and dragging calves to the branding fire, but mounted cowboys still show up at the cookhouse for breakfast well before daylight on days for working cattle. Then they join Aubrey Lange of San Angelo, who flies the helicopter that assists in gathering the cattle. Lange helps Terry Moberly, the foreman, by spotting the cattle and keeping strays from hiding in the brush to elude cowboys on the hilly terrain. Neighboring ranches that help or swap help on heavy working days include the Nail, which shares the southern boundary with the ranch. George Peacock, manager of the Nail, is a longtime friend of both Watt and Terry.

Steer calves are kept through the winter to be sold as yearlings and are shipped to market in trucks. In the earliest days, of course, cattle were driven up the trail. Later they were shipped to market in Fort Worth by rail. To accomplish this the animals were driven to the Albany railroad corrals, a trip that lasted two days. The ranch had a half-section holding pasture north of Albany and held the herd there overnight. A small building had been constructed for shelter for the crew. After World War II, hauling cattle to market became common, and the drives were discontinued. This evolution in methodology is part of the reason the ranch has made the transition into modern times and survived flood, drought, tornado, and other natural and commercial disasters.

Lambshead Ranch is a viable, working ranch that nonetheless seems caught in stasis, mostly because of the diligent effort of Watt Matthews, a man who honors the traditions of the past. In an interview he stated that he felt the best way he could honor his mother and father, whose memory he adores, is to hand the ranch over to the next generation in better shape than he received it. He has certainly worked hard to see that he does that. From his historic and animal preservation to his work with the Fort Griffin Fandangle and his board memberships in business and charitable organizations, Watt has made his mark on the ranching traditions of Texas in his own way.

The Matthews-Reynolds union from the Civil War era continues to make its mark in the modern West. Many of the ranches begun by members of this family are still being operated by descendants. Who will succeed Watt as manager of Lambshead is a decision the family corporation will decide when Watt no longer is able to make decisions and oversee the work of the ranch. The interwoven fabric of these two stalwart families still provides a unifying base of support in this cattle country along the Clear Fork.

LAMBSHEAD RANCH

Matador Land and Cattle Company

North Texas and the Panhandle

The Matador Cattle Company (forerunner of the Matador Land and Cattle Company) was founded in 1879 by five entrepreneurs: Col. Alfred Markham Britton, Henry Harrison Campbell, Spottswood W. Lomax, John W. Nichols, and Britton's brother-in-law, a man named Cata. Lomax, who had an interest in Spanish literature, is credited with selecting the name given the ranch. Some of these same men also formed the Espuela Land and Cattle Company south of the Matador.

By 1882 the ranch controlled 1.5 million acres of open range, mostly on the various tributaries of the Pease River in Motley, Floyd, Cottle, and Dickens counties west of Wichita Falls. At the time of the founding, the ranch was quite remote from any center of settlement. For example, lumber to construct the headquarters building at Ballard Springs, a site named for an early-day buffalo hunter who had his headquarters there, had to be hauled in from Fort Griffin on the Clear Fork of the Brazos River, north of Albany. The windows came by wagon from Fort Worth. The ranch continued to prosper under its founders so that, by the early 1880s, between fifteen thousand and twenty thousand calves were branded each year.

In the fall of 1882, a group of businessmen, mostly from Dundee, Scotland, bought the ranch and gave it the name Matador Land and Cattle Company. The selling price was $1.25 million. The range was stocked with approximately seventy thousand head of Longhorn cattle. Under the leadership of the Scottish investment group, the ranch prospered for almost sixty years and eventually came to include at its height of operation some three million acres in Montana, Wyoming, South Dakota, Nebraska, and Canada, along with extensive holdings in Texas. The towns of Matador and Roaring Springs were founded by the ranch. Other buildings were added to the "White House," as the headquarters came to be called. These included bunkhouses and dwellings for various supervisors and other employees living at the headquarters. A dam was also erected to form a lake from the flow of eleven springs found at the headquarters. The lake was stocked with fish, and water was used to irrigate the garden and to provide water for the house and barns. Later a large stone house on top of the hill at the headquarters replaced the original house.

The investment of Scottish capital was important to the development of the West generally, and the Scots who bought the Matador exercised strict control of the ranch. At least one member of the board visited annually, and the ranch managers reported regularly to the board, either by mail or by traveling to Scotland. Naturally, the cowboys on the range gained much to talk about from the visiting owners because the language, clothes, and personal habits were quite foreign to the Texas cattle ranges.

The Matador began fencing its ranges as early as 1884. The first fence separated Matador land from that of the Espuela Land and Cattle Company, Ltd. (later the Spur Ranch) and later from the Pitchfork and the Kit Carter outfits. These were, as one would expect, mostly boundary-marking fences, but a forty-section horse pasture was fenced off near Ballard Springs shortly thereafter. The erection of fencing continued until all of the range was enclosed and cross fencing was completed, though some early pastures contained as many as 100,000 acres.

At first in order to increase the herd, the company ordered sold each year only enough cattle to pay for the construction of wire fencing, wooden corrals, and buildings as well as to return a dividend to the stockholders. Profits were high because of seasonable range conditions and strong markets. By 1881, cattle from the Matador were shipped by rail from Colorado City, more than a hundred miles south of the headquarters, on the Texas and Pacific Railroad. Later, cattle were also shipped on the Fort Worth and Denver Railroad, which ran to Childress, and after 1885, cattle were shipped from Estelline on the Fort Worth and Denver to market in Kansas City or to ranges in the north. Following completion of the Quanah, Acme, and Pacific, the ranch shipped its cattle on it as well from Russellville and McBain. Transportation of mail and passengers from the railroad to the ranch was first done by the Matador stage-

ROARING SPRINGS

The springs were an Indian encampment for Quanah Parker's people. The ranch made good use of the water source for cattle, drinking, and occasional skinny dipping. Later when the railroad came through, a small town was established and the springs were developed into a swimming and recreation area (now privately owned).

Old Headquarters & Commissary
Matador Ranch

OLD HEADQUARTERS AND COMMISSARY

The owners from Scotland have arrived to take stock of their investment, but the derby hats and strangely cut clothes they are wearing will be the subject of many jokes in the bunkhouse tonight.

The commissary building on the left still stands in its original place on the ranch and, although the headquarters has been replaced with another finer structure, it can still be seen at the Ranching Heritage Center in Lubbock.

51

coach and later by buckboard. By 1885, the stockholders realized that overstocking the range was a problem and sold more than sixteen thousand young stocker cattle from one to three years old. This practice was common across the West at that time, and the huge numbers of cattle sold devastated the market.

Other problems were not far behind. The Matador certainly was not exempt from the devastating 1885–1887 droughts and winter storms. Losses from the storms during the winter of 1886 were estimated at more than eight thousand head. The ensuing dry period forced exploration for subsurface water and prompted widespread use of windmills and the construction of tanks to hold surface runoff for stock water. Dams were easily erected in the rolling country, which was cut by draws and canyons that favored tank construction.

In 1891, Murdo Mackenzie, a Scotsman with some background in law, insurance, and ranching in Scotland, Colorado, New Mexico, and Texas, took over the ranch and guided it with a firm hand for many years. Mackenzie became a dominant figure in ranching in the West. He had gained valuable experience working for the Prairie Cattle Company, another Scottish-owned company whose holdings ran from west of the Matador range though New Mexico and Colorado. One of his first decisions was to move the Matador company office from Fort Worth to be near his home in Trinidad, Colorado. The office was located on the second floor of the First National Bank Building in Trinidad. Mackenzie felt that having the office in that area put him in touch with the markets in Denver, where the office was later moved. More significant, being headquartered in Colorado put Mackenzie in position to appreciate and expand the ranch's holdings in northern states, which came to be extensive when ranchers found that cattle grazed on the rich northern grasses grew off better than on Texas ranges and brought better prices at marketing time. Many Matador cattle were driven to northern ranges in the early 1890s as the Matador followed the pattern of many other ranches.

Although rail transportation was available, driving was less expensive. The last long drive was in 1893 to South Dakota, a distance of nearly eight hundred miles.

Mackenzie instituted many new rules that controlled gambling and drinking by employees and required strict discipline. To control purchases by the various camps on the ranch, Mackenzie created a central commissary at Ballard Springs. One problem noted by the directors was the purchase of large quantities of raisins with seeds, which it was feared were fermented for strong drink. These changes resulted in threats to Mackenzie's life and caused the period to be a stressful one for him and the ranch.

By the turn of the century, the hold on the land leased in northern states looked uncertain, and the decision was made to purchase rather than lease grazing land. In Texas this led to the acquisition of the Alamositas, a large tract of ranch land that was part of the XIT Ranch. Its name comes from a stream in the area, located some twenty miles from Tascosa and twenty-five miles from Channing, the XIT Ranch headquarters. The Matador directors also gradually purchased Rito Blanco and other parcels near Alamositas, a total of almost 214,000 acres of what came to be called the Alamositas Division, mostly in Oldam County, in the good cattle country along the Canadian River. They also leased land known as the White Deer Lands near present-day Pampa, lands managed at one time by T. D. Hobart, a longtime manager of the JA Ranch in Palo Duro Canyon. The Texas ranch now consisted of two divisions—the Matador and the Alamositas. The latter became a holding pasture for young cattle en route to the northern ranges. In 1905 the ranch leased an additional fifty thousand acres in Canada and opened its Canadian enterprise, following the model set a year earlier in opening up the Dakota division.

Mackenzie left the ranch in 1912 to go to Brazil to run a ranch there, and John McBain, another Scot, became the fourth manager. His tenure ended with his death in 1922, at which time Mackenzie resumed control until 1936. During this time the Quanah, Acme, and Pacific Railway laid tracks across the ranch, and the management prepared to sell land to farmers along the route. The line came through the ranch, nearly ten miles south of the headquarters, so the town of Roaring Springs, the former Comanche campground and site of a ranch camp in 1879, was laid out on the line. The first train reached the townsite in June of 1913. Later a trunk line was constructed from Matador to Matador Junction, some three miles east of Roaring Springs.

During the 1920s, interest in drilling for oil struck the Matador ranges as well as other parts of the country. In 1926, when oil was booming in other parts of the country, Shell Oil Company, through a subsidiary named Roxana Petroleum Corporation, leased the mineral rights on the Matador land, but they completed no producing wells. The promise of income from oil, that mainstay of much of the Texas cattle industry, has never been of help to Matador owners. Little oil production exists today around Matador; some gas production is found near Alamositas.

In 1921, the ranch closed its Canadian division, and in 1928 bought nearly fifty thousand additional acres from the XIT, which was liquidating its holdings.

In 1940, John V. Stevens took over the Alamositas Division. In 1946 he moved to the Matador Division to become the fifth and last superintendent to run the ranch at Ballard Springs and the only man to have run both. He currently lives just west of the town of Matador and ranches part of the land he once oversaw for the Scottish stockholders.

The horse herd on the Matador came from Quarter Horse stock through Peter McQue, a fine Palomino stallion, and a son, Shiek, which served as the best-known stud for the ranch. His bloodlines were crossed with some mares showing Morgan blood as well as Thoroughbred mares and some Steel Dust mares from New Mexico to make a distinctive type of cowhorse that suited the Matador management and cowboys. Some of the horses showed too much yellow and had white eyes, so crossbreeding was undertaken to remedy the problem. The result is a heavy-bodied, medium height, strong horse suited for use in the rough Matador country. A cowboy usually had a string of a dozen of these horses to ride in the summer and at least four to ride in the winter. In some years, much of the work was done in the cold months.

Although the ranch tried some Shorthorn bulls around 1890, the management brought to the ranch some Hereford bulls. The Herefords proved superior to the Shorthorns in performance and adaptation. So the cattle on the ranges came to be big-boned Hereford cows, not purebred, and Hereford bulls that showed the right kind of size and conformation. There also was a purebred herd from which bulls were raised for the commercial herd. The best known of these Matador bulls was Prince Domino, at one time considered the finest Hereford bull alive. Domino bloodlines still figure prominently in Hereford breeding. Since the ranges at Matador were brushy, these cattle gained a well-deserved reputation for wildness and ability to hide in the thorny brush. Later, descendants were gentled, usually by patient men working with the herds and feeding them.

The ranch had provided much of the social outlet for people living on and near its range from the earliest days. Social gatherings included dances on Valentine Day and parties at Christmas and New Year's. Some of these lasted for several days, since participants had to travel long distances under difficult circumstances to attend. The social value of these gatherings was immense in a land known for isolation and loneliness, especially for the few women there. Food at these parties included various meats, lots of cakes, cookies, and other sweet items, with coffee to drink. In some years the Matador rotated hosting a Christmas party with the Slaughter and Docum ranches. The ranch also built and maintained a large swimming pool fed by the springs at Roaring Springs. This facility is now privately operated.

In 1951, the ranch held in Texas almost 800,000 acres valued at nearly $20 million. At that time a change in management in Scotland and the crunch of economic hard times brought on by the debt of World War II led to a decision to sell the ranch. Already some of the most promising land had been sold off for farming purposes. John Stevens was called to Amarillo and, on maps, divided the vast stretches into several operating units called corporations, mostly along existing fence lines. The Alamositas Division was split into the Adrian Cattle Corporation, the Alamositas Cattle Corporation, the Canadian River Cattle Corporation, the Pedrosa Cattle Corporation, and the Trujillo Cattle Corporation. The Matador Division was divided into the Bear Creek Cattle Corporation, the Dickens Cattle Corporation, the Harnica Cattle Corporation, the Mott Cattle Corporation, the Pease River Cattle Corporation, the Red Lake Cattle Corporation, the Rodatam (*Matador* spelled backward) Cattle Corporation, the Tee-Pee Cattle Corporation, the Turtle Hole Cattle Corporation, and the Wolfe Creek Cattle Corporation. The Croton pasture had already been sold to the Pitchfork Ranch at Guthrie. Names of the new units reflected, for the most part, some landmark, often a creek, located on that unit. These ranches ranged from almost a hundred thousand acres to as little as sixteen thousand acres, still a significant size for ranches in this part of Texas.

When the affairs of the breakup were settled, management donated over 400,000 items detailing the operation of the ranch over the years to the Southwest Collection at Texas Tech University in Lubbock. Other items, including the chuck wagon used on the range for many years, were given to the National Cowboy Hall of Fame in Oklahoma City.

The various ranches were bought by individuals and groups of individuals who formed business units. Many of the corporations were split up and sold in smaller parcels, but some remain intact. John Stevens, John Barnhill, and Dave Birnie of Matador and Coyal Francis, Charlie Featherston, Woodrow Featherston, Henry Grace, and Archie Lofton of Wichita Falls purchased Harnica, Turtle Hole, and Bear Creek corporations. Only Stevens and Coyal kept portions for ranching. Fred Koch, an M.I.T. graduate in chemical engineering who had made his fortune in oil, bought the Wolfe Creek, Tee-Pee, and Rodatam corporations in the name of his Rock Island Oil and Refining Company. His holdings totaled 105,000 acres. His headquarters is the original one located along the west side of Texas Highway 70, the road between Matador and Dickens just south of the town of Matador. Later, in 1971, he also bought the remaining 20,000 acres of the Yellow House Ranch, the former XIT camp that George Littlefield had purchased earlier, located near the town of Littlefield. He later sold it. For some years, Koch rented wheat fields around Plainview and other areas for grazing, a pattern widely followed by many other ranches in Texas. The Koch family donated one of the ranch headquarters buildings to the Ranching Heritage Center at Texas Tech University in Lubbock, where it is part of the outdoor exhibit in that splendid museum of Texas ranching culture. Descendants of Koch still operate the ranch. The state of Texas bought one block of the original ranch in Cottle County and turned it into a game preserve.

The heritage of this famous ranch continues through the work of men and women who knew it during its heyday and who still operate ranches on vast stretches, formerly making up both divisions. *Matador*, a Spanish word for one who kills bulls, has proved not to be a bull killer at all. The ranch with this name saw a classic line of Hereford and a particular type of Quarter Horse come into existence. These influences are still felt on the ranges in West Texas and other parts of the world where Hereford cattle and fine horses are still a necessary part of life.

MATADOR RANCH

Pitchfork Ranch

Headquarters near Guthrie

The Pitchfork Ranch traces its beginning back to 1881 when D. B. Gardner and Col. J. S. Godwin bought a herd of cattle bearing the Pitchfork brand. The original brand sported a round base; the distinctive square-cornered version developed later. The range in King and Dickens counties, watered by the South Wichita River, was open grazing at this time, but the owners filed their claims and purchased others to begin gaining ownership of the land. In 1882 Godwin sold his interest to Eugene F. Williams, and a year later A. P. Bush, Jr., of St. Louis became one of the co-owners of the ranch.

Pitchfork Land and Cattle Company, the current company, was organized in St. Louis in 1883. Stockholders were A. P. Bush, Jr., Sam J. Lazarus, D. B. Gardner, W. H. Carroll, E. F. Williams, and A. D. Brown. Brown was elected president, and Gardner became manager. Arrangements were made to buy cattle, horses, mules, wagons, and necessary equipment. The Pitchfork, or the 'Forks, as it is known locally, was a reality, and it has led in the production of fine cattle and horses for more than a century.

Management of the ranch has been remarkably stable. Gardner, the original manager, remained at his post for forty-seven productive years. He saw the original headquarters, called the Centerfire Dugout, a dwelling literally carved out of the soil, give way first in 1894 to a three-room house on Davidson Creek. Much later, a colonial ranch house would be the centerpiece of the 'Fork's headquarters. Also located there are the office, museum, cookhouse, and bunkhouse. Camps scattered around the ranch provide quarters for married cowboys who look after an assigned portion of the range. Other men in managerial positions have included Med Gardner, Press Goen, and W. H. Bryant. When A. O. "Redmud" Lambert succeeded Gardner in 1928, the ranch had nearly nine thousand cattle and five hundred horses and was just short of 115,000 acres of land.

Virgil Parr became manager in 1930. Parr was a graduate of Baylor University and Texas A&M University and had a national reputation as an agricultural economist for the U.S. government. Parr's influence was significant. He moved the ranch through difficult years from which it has emerged as a modern ranch. He put land in cultivation to grow winter wheat and oats for grazing, built a feed mill, and began to feed cattle through the droughty times. He instituted an aggressive program of cross fencing, and with a drilling machine he searched for water and dotted the ranch with watering facilities, a necessity for better breeds of cattle unable to walk long distances to water each day. Parr ran afoul of the ideas of the management and resigned in a heated board meeting in St. Louis in 1940.

In 1931, Parr hired John Stevens, a sixteen-year-old cowboy, who continued to work on the ranch and saved his money to attend Texas A&M University. During his college years he returned each summer to work on the ranch and graduated in 1937. This is the same John Stevens who would later be hired by the Matador Land and Cattle Company as one of their managers and who bore the responsibility, at the direction of the Matador's owners, of dividing that ranch when it was sold in 1951.

Rudolph Swenson was manager for two years before his accidental death in 1942. Swenson, a University of Texas graduate and the youngest of the sons of W. G. Swenson, of SMS fame, was killed in a car-train crash at Benjamin in the ranch country between Wichita Falls and Guthrie. With him in the car were Ann Carey, daughter of one of the owners, and a girl friend of hers, both of whom were coming to the ranch to ride horses and enjoy life in the open air. The two girls survived the crash.

Swenson was replaced by D. Burns, a forty-seven-year-old man with a forceful personality and good business sense. He was the brother of John Burns, manager of the Four Sixes, and a graduate of Texas A&M University. Burns continued the feeding program begun by Parr and improved the mill operation by building a large one in 1959. He established a swine operation, an unusual move for a cattle ranch in Texas. The first years of his tenure as manager were rocky ones for Burns because he lacked the support of the men working for him, and help was hard to hire during the war. In 1944, he threatened to resign if not allowed to replace men he had found uncooperative with his style of management. The board gave him the authority, and he survived this crisis, one of the sort not uncommon in ranching as it is in other kinds of business ventures. Burns' hardnosed style of management was demanding on himself and his men, but he pulled through, especially during the Korean War, when once again cowboys were hard to keep on the ranch because of the drought and the higher wages available in other jobs. Despite the problems, Burns always kept the roundups and cattle work going. Burns retired in 1965 at age seventy and remained active advising the ranch as a director of the parent company until his death in 1977.

James O'Neill Humphreys was hired by Burns in 1948 and became manager in 1965. An army veteran of World War II, Humphreys was a Texas Tech University graduate. He had some experience in banking and handling cattle in the stockyards of his native Kansas City, but he came to the ranch informally as assistant manager to Burns. He was placed in charge of the hog operation. He improved his skills by expanding that effort and making it a financially valuable part of the total operation of the ranch. He improved his management skills and his cow and horse sense in these and many other ways. Humphreys came to be considered one of the major figures in Texas agriculture before his retirement from active management in 1986. He maintained a close relationship with his university, Texas Tech, where he served on the board of directors of the Ex-student's Association and as chairman of the Ranching Heritage Center Association. In addition he was a director of the Western Cattle Raiser's Association, the American Quarter Horse Association, and the Southwestern Exposition and Livestock Show at Fort Worth.

The owners of the ranch have had a long history of active management from the St. Louis offices. In the mid 1960s, however, much change occurred following the deaths of John Gates Williams and his older brother, Eugene F. Williams. In the reorganization, Gene Williams, son of one the owners, became president of the company. Board members have included Jack Krey, operator of Krey Packing Company of St. Louis, a former president of the National Meat Institute, and a chairman of the board of the National Livestock and Meat Board. Another member was Henry Longmeyer, a man widely respected in livestock circles.

The 'Forks is widely known for quality livestock, a reputation it has worked for years to develop. One of Virgil Parr's first moves was an aggressive program for culling livestock on the ranch. He sold off the undesirable cattle, old or otherwise unsuited for breeding, and kept heifers from their own carefully selected stock. He culled all but 90 of the 324 bulls on the ranch. The original Longhorns were replaced, eventually by blooded Hereford cattle in the Prince Domino line, as well as by Mill Iron and Colorado Baldwin. D. Burns bought the prize-winning Hereford Real Onward from Nebraska as well as Royal Dundy. Later, the ranch bought bulls from the 26 Bar Ranch in Arizona owned by actor John Wayne before his death. These quality animals, by the 1930s, no longer had to make the walk to Narcisso to the railroad corral on the Quanah, Acme, and Pacific but were hauled by trucks to the railroad and, later, by larger trucks to market in Fort Worth and other marketing centers.

The ranch currently runs some registered Hereford cattle to provide bulls for its commercial herd. The commercial herd also has some Brahma blood in the cows to help give hardiness. The ranch also runs some Simbrah, a Simmental-Brahma cross gaining favor in Texas ranch circles, as well as Limousin and Beefmaster. Some black baldies—Hereford-Angus crosses—are also in the herd. The ranges of the Pitchfork require some thirty acres per cow.

Since 1969, a helicopter has been used to help round up the cattle, but the familiar cordon of cowboys is also present during these roundups. Cattle working on the 'Forks is done by the rope and drag method, as it is on the neighboring Four Sixes. Management has felt that animals are too easily hurt or distressed by the use of the working table and that the rope and drag method is best for cattle, cowboys, and horses.

When Parr began culling the cattle, he did the same with the horse herd. He carefully selected horses to be kept and sold the rest. Eventually, Thoroughbred horses were crossed with the Quarter Horse in an abortive search for the ideal Texas cowhorse. One of the first of these was My Buddy, a Thoroughbred stallion out of Gold Enamel. Later the ranch bought some Thoroughbred stallions from the U.S. government, which during the time as part of its program to provide remounts for military use made stallions available to horsemen to upgrade the quality of horse flesh in a day when the world of agriculture and war still moved by horse and mule power. These mostly Thoroughbred horses proved to be better polo ponies than cow horses, and there was much interest in the gentlemen's sport, as polo has been called, which was popular in the area mainly because of the love for the game by the St. Louis owners. One of the offsprings of the early Thoroughbred breeding was a horse named My Blue Moon, an outstanding animal that was selected to run in the Pony Express Race from Nocona, Texas, to San Francisco, California, in 1938. Most agree that the Thoroughbred cross does not produce quality cow horses.

Rudolph Swenson brought Quarter Horse blood to the ranch herd with such outstanding stallions as Seal Brown and, in 1946, Joe Bailey's King from the Four Sixes Ranch. Other stallions in the 'Forks heritage include Joe Bailey, Tiporay, Pistol Seal, Eddie Cinco, and Sir's Sir. Names familiar to almost anyone in Quarter Horse circles are found in Midland Bars, out of the famous Doc Bar line, and Reno Badger, a name reflecting the famous Gray Badger of the neighboring Four Sixes. The remuda shrank during Humphreys' years when pickups and trailers came to play a major part in the operation of the ranch. Humphreys retired the chuck wagon in 1970, but the legacy of the wagon lived on in the reputation of one of the famous cooks, Richard Bolt, whose competition in cookoffs, such as the International Cowboy Campfire Cook-Off in Abilene in the 1970s, spread his reputation over a wide area. He left his mark through a thin but important cookbook. Today about fifty mares are in the breeding herd, and the remuda of saddle horses runs close to a hundred head. The 'Forks has been famous for its gray horses with black manes and tails. The ranch has had five horse dispersal sales.

Control of mesquite and other parasitic brush is a major effort on the ranch. Early efforts were made to grub the brush by hand, but these were abandoned as impractical. Dozing with Caterpillar tractors began before World War II and escalated after the war. Aerial spraying has also been used but was abandoned because of the threat of the drifting spray to crops in the area. Various methods are still doggedly pursued in an effort to keep the range producing as much grass as possible. Although this task seems endless, only those ranches that have kept up persistent efforts have managed to wrest their ranges back from the ever-encroaching brush.

Today the ranch operates the Texas spread of some 165,000 acres divided into eighty pastures. At the insistence of D. Burns, during his day as manager, the ranch bought the Croton pasture, some 43,000 acres, controlled by the Matador Ranch. This purchase was made in 1947. The area probably gets its name from the association of the gypy water found there with the cathartic croton oil, an ill-smelling fluid indeed. It is an extremely rough pasture that was a long way from the Matador headquarters and was one of their less-used pastures. From the unusually rough Cro-

"WAITIN' FOR THE DINNER BELL"
COOKHOUSE - 1935
PITCHFORK RANCH

SALVANT

CHUCK HOUSE

The fall roundup completed, these cowboys are all back at ranch head-quarters, waiting for "Cookie" to ring the dinner bell. The chuck house is one of the oldest original structures on the ranch and, over the years, has been the scene of many a celebration, such as Christmas parties for the cowboys and their families, birthdays, and weddings, in addition to the daily serving of bountiful meals. Beyond the chuck house to the left of the painting can be seen the ranch headquarters.

58

EVENING AROUND THE CHUCK WAGON

Until recent years the chuck wagon, horse or mule drawn, would follow the roundup each spring and fall to the far reaches of the ranch and become the cowboy camp for the night. Then it would move on every few days in order to be in closer proximity to where the cowboys were working. One might say that the chuck wagon was the forerunner of today's travel trailer, for it carried everything needed on the road from food supplies to cooking-eating-cleanup utensils, first aid, and bedding. After fourteen or more hours in the saddle the cowboys thought the chuck wagon camp a mighty welcome sight. The early arrivals helped "Cookie" with preparation and the late arrivals would help clean up before bedrolls were unwrapped and scattered around the campfire. Sometimes a cowboy would entertain the others with a harmonica, and they might swap stories before all would fall exhausted into their bedrolls for the night's rest.

ton pasture, the Matador crew gathered four thousand head of wild cattle. Some of these were ten years old or older. During the drought of the 1950s, the ranch also acquired the Flag Ranch, a 31,000-acre spread, seven miles south of Laramie, Wyoming. On the ranch still run some sheep, the cowman's anathema, because the sheep eat larkspur weed, harmless to sheep but deadly to cattle. The ranch also owns a 3,900-acre spread in the famed Flint Hills of Kansas, near Eskridge, southwest of Topeka. In 1980, oil production brought to the ranch much appreciated income and led to the purchase of the 3,000-acre Jackson Ranch, on the west side of the home ranch.

The overall operation is under the direction of Eugene F. Williams, Jr., a grandson of one of the founders. Other board members are Edgar V. Dickson and John F. Krey of St. Louis, Missouri. Bob Moorhouse, son of the prominent ranching family of Togo Moorhouse, has been manager since 1986. A critically acclaimed nature photographer, Bob left the family operation to his father and brother Tom. The Moorhouse Ranch itself owns 10,000 acres in King County and leases 80,000 more in Stonewall, Borden, Knox, and Hall counties.

The 'Forks continues to occupy an important place in Texas ranch circles. Its famous brand and chuck wagon, which appears at ranch rodeos in Wichita Falls and Abilene, for example, excite the imagination of anyone familiar with ranching in the Southwest.

PITCHFORK
RANCH

60

Swenson Ranches

Headquarters in Stamford

The story of the Swenson ranches actually began in the 1850s when Swante Magnus Swenson, reputedly the first native-born Swede to set foot on Texas soil, bought railroad scrip and tracts of property in what was to become Throckmorton, Shackelford, Haskell, and Stonewall counties of West Texas. Because of the threat of Indian depredation, isolation, and lack of operating capital, this land would remain raw frontier for more than thirty years before Swenson began to operate ranches there.

Swenson had emigrated from Sweden to New York and later came to Texas, where he established himself in the mercantile business. He entered into a partnership in a plantation owned by Dr. George W. Long. Following Long's death, Swenson married Jeanette, Dr. Long's widow, and assumed control of the entire plantation. Swenson later moved to Austin and established a mercantile business in 1850. Although a successful merchant, Swenson opposed secession of Texas from the Union and, during the Civil War, had to flee Austin for Mexico. He later moved his mercantile business to New Orleans and then to New York, where he became well established in the busy financial markets of the Northeast.

In 1882 the Swenson family decided to begin ranching their vast holdings in Texas and established three ranches: Eleonora, Mount Albin, and Ericksdahl—all named for the elder Swenson's children. Eleonora became known as the Throckmorton Ranch, and Mount Albin, because of flat top hills on the ranch, became known as the Flat Top Ranch. Ericksdahl, after an early ranching history, became the site of a settlement for Swedish immigrants, who built a large Gothic-style church that still houses a Lutheran congregation and remains a well-known landmark at the site.

The ranches in Texas were not managed by the original Swenson but by his two sons, Eric and Swen Albin. They adopted the famous SMS brand that incorporated the three initials of their father. They reversed the two s's to make it distinctive and difficult to alter by rustlers. In their first trips to Texas in 1882, the Swensons established acquaintance with ranching families already there, and W. D. Reynolds, whose ranch was in Shackelford and Throckmorton counties, became a special friend. The Reynolds brothers, George and W. D., were famous cattlemen who drove herds and established ranches all over the West. Their nephew, Watkins Reynolds Matthews, still runs Lambshead Ranch. The Reynolds ranch, now owned by Ross Sloan of Breckenridge, is still in existence and borders Lambshead. Even to this day, it does not have electricity run to its vast acres along the Clear Fork. This ranch is not to be confused with the famous Long X Ranch of George Reynolds near Kent in far West Texas.

The Swensons continued to buy land. In 1883 the family bought the Ellerslie Ranch (sold in 1926) and in 1898 the ranch called Tongue River in King, Motley, and Dickens counties. Tongue River is another name for the South Pease River. Later they bought the famous Espuela Ranch. Since the name means "spur" in Spanish, the name was changed simply to the Spur or Spurs Ranch. The Spur Ranch had been founded by the same investors who began the Matador Ranch, and the same man who picked the Matador name, Spottswood Lomax, also selected the name Espuela. Over the years the Swensons sold off small parcels of land from the various ranches to pay taxes and to provide capital for expansion.

The Swenson ranches came to be a dominating influence in the cattle business generally. The family gave a section of land that was laid off to be a site for Stamford, a city that continues to be a center for ranching activity and the site of the Texas Cowboy Reunion each July. The rodeo contestants are ranch cowboys, not professional rodeo cowboys. Competition is for young and old with events from steer riding for youths to roping contests for men over the age of 60. In 1990 a Cowboy Poetry Gathering was added to accompany the Western Art Show held annually in the John Selmon Memorial Hall. A college founded there closed and

BETHEL EVANGELICAL LUTHERAN CHURCH, ERICKSDAHL COMMUNITY

"As it was in the beginning" . . . These Swedish immigrants who settled the Ericsdahl community began meeting for worship in homes and along the creek until the families of the cowboys and ranchers of the Swenson ranches built their first church in 1907. Then in 1933 they joined hands again to build a stone church, which they completed in 1942. The little white wooden church is gone now, but the beautiful stone church with the tall spire can be seen for ten miles around, a not-so-silent witness to God: ". . . is now and ever shall be."

BLACKSMITH SHOP

This scene is fast becoming a thing of the past. Blacksmiths today work primarily out of a panel truck, carrying their equipment along with them to each job. The Swenson ranches' shop is still used, located conveniently in the midst of the barn and corrals. Most of the structures are wooden construction, but the blacksmith shop is sided with corrugated tin to help keep fire from burning the shop down.

later passed its records to McMurry College, later McMurry University, in nearby Abilene. When they founded the city, the Swenson brothers donated town lots to the Texas Central Railroad to entice that line to lay tracks into Stamford from nearby Albany.

In 1911 the Swenson brothers obligated themselves for ten thousand acres of land known to contain sulphur deposits along the Texas Gulf Coast. Eric P. Swenson served as first president of the Free Port Sulphur Company, and the town of Freeport was laid out on the west side of the Brazos River. By late in 1912 the first sulphur was brought out of the mine at a dome of land called "Bryanmound." The company built Tarpon Inn in Freeport, a fine hotel resembling the Stamford Inn and the Spur Inn in West Texas. The site was abandoned in 1935 after producing five million tons of high-quality sulphur. During the time of the operation of the sulphur mines, the Swensons led in the effort to build a deep-water harbor and divert the Brazos River to feed it at what is still known as Freeport. The Dow Chemical Company took up part of the former Swenson holdings, and the Swenson returned to their ranching interests.

The Swensons became famous for their high-quality Hereford cattle. The original Longhorn cattle brought onto the ranges were crossed first with Shorthorns and later with Hereford-Shorthorn bulls. Later the Swensons would come to expect their range cattle to carry 90 percent Hereford blood with only 10 percent of the Shorthorn blood, since that seemed to provide the best conformation and other characteristics suitable to this range. Bulls on the ranch for many years were offspring from a nucleus of a hundred Hereford heifers, purchased by the ranch in the early 1900s. Careful selection and breeding practices and the selection of herd bulls brought about ranch-raised cattle that became a standard in the market place.

The Swensons, under the direction of Frank Hastings, pioneered mail order buying of cattle, where buyers did not have to see the cattle before purchasing. To succeed at this the ranch had to maintain its reputation for top-quality cattle. Later they began selling cattle by the pound instead of by the head, at the time a novel approach to marketing cattle. Another practice credited to the ranch was that of dehorning young cattle when they were branded in order to eliminate the dangerous horns when the larger animals were put into feed lots. In the late 1960s and early 1970s, the herd reached twenty thousand head, with slightly less than half being mother cows. The rest were calves, yearlings, and bulls.

The Swenson horse herd traces from Arab, a pure white Arabian stallion bought by Alfred Dyer, a close associate of the family and the first manager of the Swenson ranches. This famous sire was crossed with a band of fifty Mexican mares, horses that had innate cow-sense. Later offspring were crossed with standard bred horses, Thoroughbreds, Morgans, and other strains. The mostly white or gray Swenson horses became widely known. Famous horses from the line include Swen Miss 16, a junior champion cutting horse; and Red Boy, a cutting horse trained by Milt Bennett, which won many honors for the Swensons in the 1950s. The remuda of saddle horses at one time numbered slightly less than two hundred. Horses are still raised on the ranch, some to use and a few to sell. Some of the brood mares trace back to Hollywood Gold, a famous early sire of the 6666 Ranch. Today the stallion, Fly Cee Two, a stud out of the famous Three Bars, a fine Quarter Horse, is run with the band of mares.

Extensive efforts were made in the 1940s to eradicate parasitic growths of prickly pear and mesquite trees by bulldozing brush on Swenson ranges. Because of this effort, SMS ranges were remarkably free of the growths for many years. Financing for this operation came from extensive oil production on the ranches. Once the ranges were cleared, the ranch kept tractors in the pastures for several years,

64

rooting out the pesky plants. Their range conservation program has proved that more cattle can be ranged on grasslands kept free of the moisture-robbing mesquite and the thorny prickly pear. The efforts have continued into the present, depending upon cash flow, cattle prices, and other such factors. Controlled burning is also a technique used to control the brush.

Individuals important to the ranch have been many. Among the Swensons are Carl and Gene Swenson, presidents in the early 1970s. Gene was president of the Texas Cowboy Reunion, Inc., from 1959 to 1989. Willie Gustaf Swenson was the first president of the Texas Cowboy Reunion. One of the most interesting non-Swensons in ranch history was Scandalous John Selmon, who earned his name by complimenting the "scandalous" way a horse named Old Tallow Face could buck. John was the nephew of John Selmon, a gunman who had killed John Wesley Hardin in El Paso years earlier. Others include Clifford Eugene "Poss" Murray, foreman of the Throckmorton Ranch, and his son, Davis E. "Wendy" Murray, a later foreman of the Throckmorton Ranch; W. H. "Kid" Bacot, a foreman of Tongue River Ranch; Billy Smith, foreman of the Flat Top Ranch; and Taylor Martin, a later foreman of Tongue River Ranch.

One recent way that the business acumen of the Swenson Company is evident is the commercial beef outlet owned by the Swen R. Swenson Cattle Company in Stamford. Located just west of the square is Swenson Meats, Inc., where carefully selected, fed, slaughtered, and packaged beef bearing the SMS Brand is marketed. In this way, the ranch gets the profit of the rancher, the feedlot operator, and the commercial distributor, certainly a good way to control quality and bring an outstanding product to the consumer.

By the mid-1970s the Swenson ranches operated three units that comprised more than 225,000 acres of land. The Spur Ranch was sold off. Those remaining were Flat Top Ranch's 40,718 acres northwest of Stamford, Tongue River Ranch's 79,141 acres lying between Matador and Paducah, and Throckmorton Ranch's 106,000 acres between Throckmorton and Seymour. In 1978 the heirs of the Swenson Land and Cattle Company divided the ranch into four companies: Swen R. Swenson Cattle Company, Tongue River Ranch Company, Throckmorton Land and Cattle Company, and SMS Ranch Company. In the mid-1980s, the SMS Ranch Company sold its holdings to Lester Clark of Breckenridge and took in trade a ranch that Clark owned in South Dakota. The land now under the Swenson name is still controlled by members of the Swenson family. Swen R. Swenson Cattle Company kept the original brand. One of the other ranches brands the Spur Brand, which they kept when they sold the Spur Ranch properties, and another brands the TLC connected.

The ranch operation is complex, but a closer look at the Swen R. Swenson Cattle Company serves to illustrate the kind of operation now underway. The stock is watered from wells and tanks, and the intermittent flow of Paint Creek and the Salt Fork of the Brazos River runs through the ranch. In this country it takes twenty-five to thirty, and even in some areas thirty-five acres, per cow. Gary Mathis, a Texas Tech University graduate and former director of the Texas A&M Experiment Station on Swenson land near Throckmorton, manages the Swen R. Swenson Ranch. In addition to his duties as ranch manager, Mathis replaced Gene Swenson as president of the Texas Cowboy Reunion Association.

The operation of the Swen R. Swenson Ranch requires six cowboys, who work under the direction of Billy Smith, longtime foreman at the ranch. He was a Swenson employee first in 1941; following his military service in World War II, he rejoined the ranch and has worked there since that time. Presently, only two companies of the Swenson properties run their operations out of the distinctive Swenson Building in downtown Stamford, just one block east of the square. This building has the appearance of an earlier day in ranching. Its hardwood floors are worn and dented by the rowels of spurs across its timbers. One can smell horse sweat and almost hear spurs jingling in this traditional setting. In addition, three full-time farmers till between six and seven thousand acres that grow sorghum and winter wheat. Cattle are grazed on the wheat in the winter, and the sorghum is baled for feeding to the cattle grazing the wheat when necessary and to other cattle on the ranch during icy weather. Cattle on the ranch are worked on mechanical tables, not roped and dragged, and are gathered by cowboys in the traditional way, without the benefit of helicopter. Cowboys do trailer their horses to the pastures to be worked, as is the practice across ranch country.

Horses on the ranch are broken when they are two years old by one man who does that kind of work for them. Rather than bucking out the horses, he uses his skill to gentle the horses by first driving them and trotting them in the round pen before he rides them. There are currently eight mares in the mare band, down from eighteen in 1989. The ranch simply no longer requires that many horses to run the operation. The ranch sells part of the fillies but will keep one or two a year to replace old mares.

The influence of the Swenson Land and Cattle Company has long been, and continues to be, a pivotal force in the area around Stamford and across the state, and literally across the nation in the distribution of its fine cattle. Active in the formation of the Cowboy Hall of Fame in Oklahoma City, in the Texas Cowboy Reunion at Stamford, in the bringing of rail transportation to that section of Texas, and in the founding of a deep-water port on the coast, the descendants of a Swedish immigrant who came to the United States and lived out the American dream continue to make a mark on ranching.

SWENSON RANCH

Waggoner Ranch

Headquarters near Vernon

The Waggoner Ranch, which contains well over a half million acres of predominantly flat ranch country in North Texas near Wichita Falls, is located in Wilbarger, Wichita, Knox, Foard, Archer, and Baylor counties. The main headquarters is near Vernon. It is one of the oldest and certainly one of the best operated and productive ranches in this part of the world. The ranch originally branded three reversed D's in a string but later adopted the single reversed D. Because of this early brand, the ranch sometimes is referred to as the Triple D or Three D.

The story of the founding of the ranch is epic in scope. W. T. (Tom) Waggoner and his father, Dan, had several small herds of cattle in North Texas, but the real boost of W. T. into ranching on the scale that he desired came in 1866 when, still a teenager, he bossed a drive of six thousand Longhorn steers from Clay County in North Central Texas to the railhead in Kansas. He and his father came home with $55,000 in cash.

Tom married Ella Halsell, whose family was important in Texas ranching, and moved to the area where China Creek joins the Red River. He and his father bought thirty miles of river-front land stretching from China Creek to Pease River. They also leased thousands of acres of land in Indian Territory, now the state of Oklahoma, across the Red River. Always looking ahead, Tom was not surprised in 1900 when changes in federal laws ended the policies governing the laws of the Oklahoma lands. He hired Robert L. More, a young man from the region who was an expert in abstracts, and set him to buying property in the area. Dan died in 1902, but by 1903 Tom had put together a half-million-acre ranch, roughly thirty-five miles by twenty-five miles in size. He set about improving the land as best he could and stocking it with the best cattle he could obtain. During the Great Depression, he bought an additional 160,000 acres of ranch land near Mosquero, New Mexico. This ranch served for a time as a range for steers.

In 1909 Tom divided the ranch in quarters and gave equal parts to the three children: Electra (1882–1925), Guy Leslie (1883–1950), and E. Paul (1889–1967). He kept the other himself. By 1923, eleven years before his death, he had consolidated the holdings into the now-famous W. T. Waggoner Estate. The present owners are Electra Waggoner Biggs, Mrs. Biggs' two daughters and sons-in-law, and her grandchildren, who own one-half of the ranch; and A. B. "Bucky" Wharton III, grandson of Electra Waggoner Wharton and great-grandson of W. T. Waggoner.

The Waggoners bought and sold a considerable amount of property in building the ranch. One of their efforts led to the establishment of the Waggoner Colony in Wilbarger County. This land, suitable for farming, was sold at $15.00 an acre. This money was used to purchase 100,000 acres of land on the Wichita River at $5.00 per acre. The new land joined other Waggoner holdings and helped consolidate the property.

Tom Waggoner's insight into ranching and his ability to solve problems facing ranches have been major strengths of the operation. The ranch has also been fortunate to have additional leadership. Like Robert Kleberg, who married into the King family and guided that ranch for many years, the Waggoners came under the direction of John Biggs, who had married Electra Waggoner, E. Paul's daughter, after the couple met during World War II in New York, where she was studying art. Biggs, a native of Sherman, Texas, had attended Virginia Military Institute and had done graduate work at the University of Maine. He had a chance at a career in professional baseball with the New York Giants but took a job instead with International Paper Company. He secured leave from International Paper and served in the Office of Price Administration during 1941 and entered military service in 1942. At the time of his discharge in 1946, he was a lieutenant colonel in the Quartermaster Corps. Biggs became assistant manager of the Waggoner in 1946.

ROUNDUP AT THE RANCH

Branding was a unique experience for this city-bred artist. Six men in less than twenty seconds' time branded, gave shots to, dehorned, castrated, clipped the ear of, and tagged a calf. Meanwhile, the wrangler was roping the next calf to be treated. Two teams and two wranglers working all day could treat about two thousand calves.

The Waggoner Ranch has the distinction of being the first to use helicopters for rounding up cattle, "riding fence," and so on, and own their own copters.

HORSE STABLE WITH POCO BUENO

One of the most unique buildings on the Waggoner Ranch is its horse stable. Built of colorful native sandstone, its unusual shape draws immediate attention. The second-level windows were designed to represent the Waggoner brand, the reverse "D."

From the beginning the ranch has enjoyed world recognition for its Quarter Horse stock. Probably the most famous of all was Poco Bueno, a halter and cutting horse champion. He sired many well-known Quarter Horses that became champions in their own right. Today his grave and monument are prominently displayed just across the highway from the entrance to Zacaweista, the main ranch headquarters.

Mrs. Biggs, a talented sculptress, produced works of such political figures as Dwight David Eisenhower, Harry Truman, and John Nance Garner and other such figures as Texas actress Mary Martin, famous for her role as Peter Pan and in *South Pacific*, the King Ranch's Robert Kleberg, and comedian Bob Hope. Perhaps her best-known piece in the Southwest is a statue of Will Rogers on Soap Suds, his favorite horse. Casts of the statue are visible outside the Will Rogers Coliseum in Fort Worth and at the entrance of Texas Tech University in Lubbock.

Other able managers have come along as well. Richard G. "Dick" Yeager, manager from 1975 to his death in 1990, graduated from Oklahoma State University with a degree in agriculture education in 1951. After teaching and working in agri-related activities for several years, he took a job as assistant farm manager for the Waggoners in 1964. By 1975 he was farm and ranch manager. He met and married his wife, Rosalla Sykora, while at Oklahoma State. Their son-in-law, Tandy Whitehead, a U.S. Army veteran, flies a helicopter on the ranch. Yeager assisted Charles Prather, who was general manager and trustee of the Waggoner Estate. Yeager had working for him an assistant ranch manager, an assistant farm manager, and an assistant manager for the horse operation. Yeager was succeeded by Jimmy Smith, the present manager.

The Waggoner Ranch has fortunately had the benefit of wealth generated by oil production. In a 1903 effort to drill a deep well in search of artesian water, the driller brought oil to the surface, much to the disgust of Tom, who had hoped for water. Later Will Rogers, who was a frequent visitor to the ranch, would say that, on the Waggoner, each cow had forty acres of grass and an oil well of her own. To aid in the marketing of the oil, the Waggoners built an oil refinery near Electra.

Various personalities other than the Waggoners have been important to the ranch. Shinnery McElroy, an old-time cowboy, began serving with the Waggoners in 1879. In his older years he farmed some of the property still in the Waggoner Colony. Tony Hazlewood worked for the Waggoners for fifty years, most of those years as foreman, and is buried at Zacaweista, the main headquarters outside Electra. Burton Williams was a cowboy from the late 1930s and became a cook in the early 1960s. Fred Albright ran the wagon and branding crews for many years. In 1990, Paul Whitley, at age 86, still lived in his retirement at Cedar Top Camp on the ranch. It is fair to say that often people began working for the Waggoners and were so impressed with the skill with which the operation was run and the care taken with the employees that many have served the Waggoners for long years.

The Hereford cattle on the Waggoner have long been known for high quality. Like most early ranches, the Waggoner tried crossing Texas, or Longhorn, cattle with Shorthorns but eventually settled on Herefords. For many years the ranch bought champion bulls at the Denver Livestock Show. These were supplemented with bulls bought in Colorado, Iowa, Kansas, Oklahoma, Wyoming, Michigan, Illinois, and Texas. More recently, some crossbreeding has been tried with Brangus, Simbrah, and Angus, as well as Brahma, but Hereford remains the basic breed.

Railroad shipping of cattle during the 1930s was from Oklaunion on the Fort Worth and Denver Railroad and at Fulda on the Wichita Valley Railroad. Later, as on other ranches, trucks came to be used, and each camp is now equipped with modern shipping pens to accommodate the huge vans.

In order to improve ranges for the cattle, the Waggoners went to much trouble to kill the mesquite trees, principally by use in the early days of kerosene. After the trees had died, they were knocked down with a large roller. The large wood was used as fuel, and the lighter wood was piled with prickly pear, which was cut off level with the ground. When these piles dried, they were burned.

In the early 1970s use of the chuck wagon on roundups was discontinued. Today, under the supervision of Jim Patterson, who still holds the title of Wagon Boss, a crew of about a dozen cowboys works the cattle. Patterson is responsible for seeing that his men get the work done smoothly and quickly and with as little disruption of the cattle as possible. Living at the headquarters, these men haul their horses to pastures to be worked each day. They are joined there by the man who lives in the camp that has jurisdiction over that pasture. Each of the regular hands has six or seven horses assigned to him to ride in rotation. This number is down from a dozen or so assigned to each man when the wagon was still in operation.

Camp names are White Face, Electra Lake, McDuff, Kite, La Paloma, Fluida, Alamosa, Sam Jones, Self Place, Cedar Top, McLardy, Harts, Dee's, Santa Rosa, Four Corners, and Zacaweista, the headquarters. These are located across the vast acreage in order to have men positioned to see after the various parts of the range.

The Waggoners were among the first to use the helicopter to herd cattle. In June of 1953 they purchased a Bell helicopter for this use. In addition to its use in supporting the cowboys in roundups, the helicopter has been used to check fences and water sources, survey wild game, hunt predators, and check on oil leases. The Waggoners have continued to lead in the use of the helicopter to gather cattle. Now when the cattle hear the popping buzz of the rotor, they head to the pens. The animals stay ahead of a cordon of cowboys mounted on fine Waggoner Quarter Horses.

Horses have been an important part of the Waggoner operation from the beginning, and world recognition has come to the Waggoners' Quarter Horses. A famous Waggoner Quarter Horse was Yellow Jacket, a Palomino stallion, which sired Cow Puncher—W. T. Waggoner's favorite horse. Other famous horses in the line were Yellow Wolfe and Yellow Bear.

Another famous Quarter Horse was Poco Bueno, one of the best of all Quarter Horses. A halter and cutting horse champion, the horse was bought as a colt by E. Paul Waggoner from Jess Hankins of San Angelo in 1945. In the next decade this horse established his name and that of the Waggoners throughout the show and cutting world. As a stud he was unsurpassed in passing along desirable characteristics to his offspring. These included such well-known animals as Poco Tivino, Poco Mona, Poco Lena, Poco Champ, Poco Dell, Poco Stampede, and a host of others.

Other studs have included Rainy Day, Midnight, Pretty Boy, Cotton-Eyed Joe, and Doctor Mac. At one time, five hundred foals a year were born on the Waggoner Ranch. In the early 1970s, the Waggoners kept thirty-one stallions and foaled about two hundred colts a year. Currently, that number of foals has been reduced to about fifty or sixty per year.

In the late 1960s the Waggoners kept three men working in the bronc pens breaking geldings for ranch use. When the horses had been ridden enough that they would accept the saddle, the hands would gather a string of these green-broke broncs and drive them to where the wagon was camped on the roundup. There the foreman would parcel out the horses to the men to ride. These were large, big-boned, spirited horses, and the men had to be on their toes at all times to ride them.

The lure of good horse flesh did not stop with the Quarter Horse. Tom Waggoner was particularly enamored with the sport of kings—the race track—and sought to breed the best possible Thoroughbred horses. He established a horse breeding farm at Arlington, sixteen miles east of Fort Worth. An outlay of $1.5 million set up this twenty-five-acre operation. It was equipped with a brood barn and three rooms especially designed for foaling. These were heated to ensure that colts born during cold weather would not be chilled. This kind of facility was unusual in Texas at the time. Tom's love of racing caused him to pour two million

Depression-era dollars into developing a race track called Arlington Downs between Fort Worth and Dallas. He succeeded in getting pari-mutuel betting approved in 1933. This short-lived period soon ended, however, and legal betting was not returned to Texas until the late 1980s.

The famous red, white, and blue silks of the Waggoner racing stables sped to fame with such now almost forgotten names as Chuck Wagon, Money Getter, Strideway, Quatrae Bras II, and Kerrio. Among the famous Waggoner Thoroughbred studs were Phlaros, Liberty Limited, Kilkerry, and Royal Ford. Among the mare band were Handy Mandy, Canfli, Girl Scout, That's That, and Pansy Walker.

The Waggoner Ranch is one of the finest in the true tradition of western ranches. Its interest in the land and cattle and in fine horses is unsurpassed. The abundance of oil wealth has brought within the grasp of the family many opportunities denied those whose property did not have this source of revenue. The remarkable saga of the Waggoner Estate continues to this day. Their teams regularly compete in the Texas Ranch Roundup, a ranch rodeo at Wichita Falls, and their leadership in this activity is widely acknowledged. In 1990, the team won the event for the third successive year and was awarded permanent control of the trophy called "Rocks 'n Hard Places" by artist Lex Graham. Their cowboys are still among the finest to be found, and their horses are considered the best available anywhere.

WAGGONER RANCH

XIT Ranch

Western Edge of the Texas Panhandle

One of the largest ranches ever in the United States is the now-defunct XIT, whose more than three million acres once spread along a two-hundred-mile stretch up the western side of the Texas Panhandle. Counties covered included all or parts of Hockley, Cochran, Lamb, Bailey, Castro, Parmer, Deaf Smith, Oldham, Hartley, and Dallam, to make up the traditional "Ten in Texas" erroneously thought to be indicated by the brand. Towns on the old range include Buffalo Springs, Texline, Dalhart, Channing, Bovina (originally known as Bull Town), and Spring Lake.

Of its origins, C. L. Douglas writes, "The XIT built the Texas State House: The State of Texas built the XIT" (p. 322). Actually, the state traded the three million acres it had set aside for the purpose to a firm from Chicago—Taylor, Babcock and Company—to build the second-largest state house in the United States. In March of 1882, a representative of the firm, Mr. A. C. Babcock, went to the Panhandle cowtown of Tascosa, then just a motley collection of buildings. There he gathered an entourage of a few cowboys, a surveyor named W. S. Mabry, the county clerk named Mr. Vivian, some vehicles including an army ambulance for himself, and two wagons; and the group set off to see the property. The chuck wagon was loaded with supplies, including wood from a large dead cottonwood tree. Later prairie coal, dried cattle and buffalo droppings, which came to be called "Babcock's coal" because of Babcock's strong aversion to food cooked over it, was the only source available since wood is a scarce commodity in the Texas Panhandle. Then was launched one of the most famous Texas ranches. The surveying of property turned into a veritable odyssey for the men involved. Even though the company had accepted the three million acres sight unseen, they had every reason to know or to believe they knew the kind of country they had.

The company traded for the land with full intentions of selling it off in small portions for development into farms and ranches. Various circumstances prevented their doing that early enough for that option to be practical, so they decided to convert the entire piece of property into a large ranch. Because of their desire to control access to the property, the decision was made to fence the entire tract. Required were 260 miles of fence on the west, 275 miles on the east side with its many turns, and about 40 across the ends. In all, with this fencing and some interior fencing with four strands of barbed wire attached to cedar posts, the wire, if stretched in a single line, would have covered 6,000 miles. Needed materials made up 300 rail carloads, one carload alone being gate hinges. The cost was $181,000. Eventually the ranch was divided into ninety-four different pastures. So large was the ranch that it had an express rider to carry mail and news across it, a ranch store, and even its own license to sell tobacco. Establishment of the ranch constituted a major business boom to the Panhandle, simply from shipping supplies to such a large operation.

To secure the capital needed for purchasing cattle, windmills, and supplies, as well as constructing houses and paying for labor, John Farwell, one of the directors of the parent company and after whom a Panhandle town was named, founded the Capital Freehold Land and Investment Company, Ltd., and financed it largely with pounds sterling generated on a trip to England in 1885. Farwell himself became managing director of the company and named Col. B. H. Campbell, known as "Barbecue" because of his BQ brand, as manager. The ranch adopted its brand at the suggestion of a former trail driver named Ab Blocker, a Concho River country rancher who brought the first herd of stocker cattle to the ranch. Requirements for the brand were that it would be easily applied, readily identifiable, and put on with a single bar of scorching-hot iron. Another requirement was that it not be easily altered by rustlers. The cattle were branded XIT on the side with the year brand on the shoulder, and the number of the division on which the animal was born was branded on the jaw.

Other stock on the ranch in the earliest days came from the coastal plains of Texas, from C. C. Slaughter's Lazy S Ranch, and others. By November of 1886, well over 100,000 head of cattle stocked the XIT, and several hundred miles of fence had been constructed. J. Evetts Haley states that seven divisions made up the original ranch: Buffalo Springs, Middle Water, Ojo Bravo, Rito Blanco, Escarbada, Spring Lake, and Las Casas Amarillas, commonly called Yellow Houses (p. 147).

In 1887, Campbell was removed as manager, and A. L. Matlock, an attorney from back East, took control. His methods were harsh and quite different from those of Campbell, and he made many enemies. By the time the capitol in Austin was completed in 1888 at a cost of $3,224,593, the ranch had 125,000 head of cattle on its vast stretches of grasses. The calves were roped and dragged to the fire, because in those days what pens were available were great distances apart. It made little sense to undergo long drives just to pen the cattle when the numerous cowboys—well over one hundred scattered over the ranch—could handle the work just fine on the open range. In the winter, when cattle work was slow, the cowboys often hunted dangerous lobo wolves and were paid a bounty to kill the animals, which had voracious appetites for livestock. Many of the men made more money from hunting and skinning wolves than they did from working as cowboys.

The original cattle were mostly Longhorn, but after 1887, crossbreeding of Longhorn stock with Herefords, Durhams, and polled Angus, brought in from Illinois, Iowa, and Missouri, resulted in cattle better suited to producing beef in this climate with its hot, dry periods but icy winter storms.

Sufficient water for stock was a crucial problem for the ranch in its early stages, and available underground sources were insufficient. Tanks were scraped out and dams erected by cowboys using teams of mules. When the men discovered that the shallow tanks went dry quickly following the scant rains, they tried applying thin layers of cement and, later, smearing the ground in the tank beds with tar. Still later they plowed the ground and then herded cattle onto the dirt to pack it tightly. Cowboys had to keep the animals on the site until the job was done. And then in one of nu-

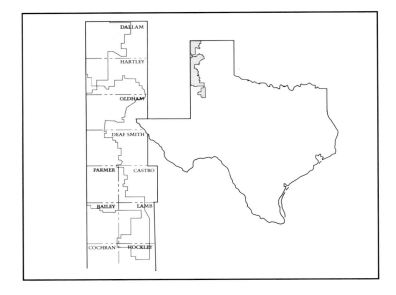

merous innovations brought to the ranch, salt blocks, a necessary ingredient for cattle productivity, were placed on the tank beds, and the cattle eventually compacted the soil by milling there. Not until 1910 was a water well of sufficient production drilled, and by then a pump of sufficient strength to run it was available. This was too late for the XIT in its glory days, but the discovery created a productive agricultural area.

One of the problems that faced the ranch every winter was range fires. With few natural barriers to this onslaught, the ranch was vulnerable to the effects of the fire carried by high winds common in the area. In those days when feeding of cattle was unknown and impracticable, burned range land meant the end of the operation. Various efforts were tried to reduce the threat. One of these was plowing a firebreak completely around the ranch. This included plowing two furrows some distance apart and then, at the appropriate time, burning off the ground in between to provide a firebreak.

The most famous fire on the XIT, labeled "the big burn," swept a path from seventy to one hundred miles wide and one hundred miles long across the ranch in December of 1894. Though the source of the fire is not know for certain, it is suspected that a disgruntled cowboy tossed a single match into a rat nest on a day when he assumed, even before modern weather forecasting techniques were developed, that the wind shifts would cause the fire to spread in the most destructive possible direction.

The citizens of Tascosa watched with interest as the XIT came to the Panhandle. Situated along the sandy banks of the Canadian River, the town drew men—and the kind of women they sought—to the cattle country where open range was still a reality. Cattle of the T Anchor and LS Ranches roamed at will. The management of the XIT was rigorous in its enforcement of a series of rules about uses of XIT resources. Management insisted that the cowboys and section foremen charge travelers who stopped for help for necessary supplies, such as food and grain. The ranch also created a lot of enemies among the men that it fired for sometimes minor infractions of unreasonable rules. These men still hung around Tascosa and posed a threat to retaliate by starting range fires, rustling cattle, and cutting fences.

For these and other reasons, when the railroad started across the Panhandle of Texas, XIT officials offered incentives and applied political pressure for the railroad to bypass Tascosa and created instead the XIT town of Channing, which later became the ranch headquarters. The railroad made and broke many a promising town, and the Tascosa-Channing example is not unusual except that Channing is still a small point on a rail line. Tascosa died as a town, and its buildings were taken over to provide facilities for Cal Farley's Boys Ranch.

Grass-fat cattle from Texas did not bring as much on the Chicago market as did those finished on the nutritious grasses of the Northern Plains. In 1889, the ranch leased rangeland in the Black Hills of South Dakota. Later, officials bought land about sixty miles north of Miles City, Montana, between the Yellowstone and Missouri rivers and leased two million additional acres of grassland. In 1890,

the first drive to the Montana range, a trip of 850 miles across Colorado and Wyoming, consisted of ten thousand steers divided into four herds, spaced at least two days apart. Though rail shipment was available, and the railroads were upset that the ranch did not use it, trailing was cheaper. So the chuck wagons came out and a herd of three hundred horses was assembled to carry the cowboys who would drive the stock to the northern ranges.

A fenced piece of land so enormous was a serious impediment to migration across the Texas Panhandle and into New Mexico. More than one traveler was missput by the XIT fences and was hostile when, as he crossed and spent the night at one of the camps, he was asked to pay in cash for food for himself or grain for his horses. The management of the XIT was not inclined to "neighbor" well in the fashion of that day in that part of the world. This, too, would cause them problems in the long run. Former XIT cowboys living in and around the town of Hartley made it also a hot-bed of resentment against XIT management, even bringing A. G. Boyce, one of the managers, to trial for rustling in a cleverly designed plan of planting marked cattle in the XIT herds.

The ranch was not able to operate without becoming involved in politics. Some members of the group were in politics on a national level, but more problems developed for the ranch at the local level. Eventually, county records at Hartley Station were carried in a wagon in the dark of night to Channing, and the county seat was moved to the XIT town.

The hostility toward the ranch was growing in the form of burned rangeland, rustled cattle, and cut fences. In its typical fashion at that time, the ranch decided to cope with the problem by hiring gun hands, some of them former Texas Rangers. This policy, however, was ineffective. In a definite change of direction, XIT aloofness ended. The management sent word to allow the neighbors to turn cattle in on XIT grass when the adjoining pastures burned; XIT cowboys were encouraged to help their neighbors. Dances were held on the ranch, and a new spirit of cooperation was evident.

75

Stage Stop
Dalhart to Tucumcari!
XIT Ranch

STAGE STOP, ATASCOSA DIVISION

Nothing stands here now, overlooking the valley that leads to the Canadian River, except a few foundation stones, some broken axles, and other wheel parts—silent witnesses to the bone-crushing journey between Dalhart and Tucumcari a hundred years ago. This was not a stop for meals or a bed for the night but merely a place to repair damages incurred on the road filled with boulders, logs, and chuckholes. While repairs were being made, the passengers had time to get a drink of cool water, walk about, and take time to enjoy the view before heading north once again toward Dalhart.

"PAYDAY"
HEADQUARTERS
XIT RANCH
CHANNING, TEXAS

HEADQUARTERS

The business office, built in 1890, is located across from the Fort Worth and Denver Railroad in the town of Channing. It was the place where records were kept and payrolls were made for the entire three-million-acre ranch. The ranch consisted of seven divisions and ran two hundred miles along the western side of the Panhandle from Oklahoma on the north to west of Lubbock on the South. For all its size, and maybe because of it, the ranch basically lasted only fifteen years, but it will always remain in the hearts and memories of Texans.

The failure to produce economic return promised to the British investors caused the British syndicate to lose interest noticeably by 1888. It was not until 1915 that the members of the syndicate were paid and the unit dissolved.

In 1901, a final stage of change began. In the sixteen years the ranch had existed, it had shown no profit. The conclusion drawn by the management was that the ranch was simply too large to operate effectively. Farwell decided to keep 367,732 acres in the Yellow Houses division and put the rest up for sale. By 1903 the price of land had risen to $5.00 per acre. George W. Littlefield, a famous West Texas personality, purchased 236,000 acres of land, and the Matador Ranch to the east purchased 200,000 acres. In the first year of sale, over a million acres, one third of the total property, were sold. By 1912, the ranch had sold the stock and equipment and had leased its remaining land to two men named Shelton and Trigg. The XIT, the biggest ranch in what was then the biggest state, was no more. By 1950 only 20,000 acres remained of the initial 3 million. Capital Mineral Rights Company of Chicago, the only remnant of the original company, still holds mineral rights under some of the property.

For all its size and importance, the XIT was temporary by design. During its quarter century of life it loomed large in the minds and hearts—the myth, if you will—of Texas ranching. The XIT is alive and well in the minds of many. Cattle wearing other brands still roam the former holdings, and a rodeo in its name is held at Dalhart each summer. The headquarters building at Channing is being restored by owners Bill and Patricia Kirkemende.

Although the XIT is gone, the State House in Austin stands like a granite monument to the ranch its construction created. One of the unique features of this story is the immensity in all areas—the gigantic ranch and the huge seat of legislature. This bigness epitomizes Texas to many, but it was the bigness of the XIT that caused its downfall. It proved that one could own too much land to manage effectively. Texans do not like that lesson, but reality is a relentless teacher. It is difficult to care for a hundred thousand head of cattle in an ice storm that denies grazing to the herd and freezes its scant water supplies or fight a grass fire on a one-hundred-mile front. It is impossible to control the politics in ten counties so that fair treatment comes to what is seen as an oppressive absentee landlord. For these and other reasons the XIT is a better memory than it was a reality. But to many a cowboy who could really "let his feet down" on the long miles to ride across open range land, it is still a psychological loss to him and to the rest of us.

'XIT'

XIT RANCH

Y.O. Ranch

Hill Country near Mountain Home and Kerrville

The story of the famous Y.O. Ranch, headquartered in the rocky, rugged, but scenic Hill Country of the state near Mountain Home, is one of the most romantic in the history of ranching. The spread was founded by Charles Armand Schreiner, certainly one of the giants of ranching in the West. Having come with his parents from Alsace-Lorraine, he was orphaned early when his father, Gustave Adolph, died and left a wife and five children. Within five years his mother, Charlotte, was also dead. The children were scattered, and one later died at the hands of Confederate vigilantes.

By the time Charles Schreiner was fourteen in 1854, he had enlisted in the Texas Rangers, even though he was below legal age. In his travels with the Rangers he saw the wooded canyons along the Guadalupe River in the Hill Country and decided that this would be his home when he left service with the famous frontier law officers.

Schreiner was a man of conviction. By 1858 he had a small ranch in the Hill Country along Turtle Creek. He briefly opened a store that served a few settlers and an army post at Camp Verde, the site of the army's abortive attempt at using camels as beasts of burden in the Southwest. After his service in the Civil War, Schreiner was discharged from Scott's Brigade in San Antonio and walked to his place on Turtle Creek. Along with all other Texans he faced difficult straits but survived. Four years later he moved to Kerrville, now a scenic and thriving town but then hardly a village, which would later serve as a shipping point for his cattle. He was elected county and district clerk, but more significant, he opened a store with August Faltin. Schreiner proved an astute storekeeper, and he stayed at this work as part of his efforts as long as he was able before passing it on to his sons, whom he regularly supervised until his death. The store did a considerable volume of business, but there was little money in Texas at the time. Most of the trade was in hides and other goods, such as shingles split from cypress trees growing along the river. When trail herds from Texas began to be driven to Kansas and sold, the result was cash, often gold, brought back to Texas. And some of this found its way into Schreiner's business. Because of the income, he set up a bank, which his son L. A. ran for decades.

Impressed with the money made in the cattle business, Schreiner began buying inexpensive land in the Hill Country. Always careful, he depended on his mercantile business to get him through the hard times, particularly the disastrous period of 1886–1888 when most cattlemen in the West went broke. Nonetheless, Schreiner doggedly persisted in establishing himself in the cattle business. His famous Y.O. brand came with cattle bought from J. W. Taylor and James Clements, partners in Goliad County. Taylor is well known as part of the Taylor-Sutton feuding families from that part of Texas.

Charles Schreiner Wool and Mohair Company bought and sold huge amounts of wool and mohair through mercantile outlets. Schreiner also dealt in such items as pecans, eggs, and poultry—any items that would generate cash. He had, in addition, a grist mill, a saw mill, a cotton gin, an electric power plant, and a water works. In 1898, he incorporated his operation with his sons A. C., L. A., and Gus as officers. His family now also included younger children, Charles A., Jr., Walter, and three daughters, Lena, Frances, and Mimi. Schreiner also saw the need for higher education in the Hill Country and established Schreiner Institute, later called Schreiner College, a junior college that is now a four-year institution.

By 1919, Schreiner had accumulated impressive holdings in ranch land. These included the Live Oak Ranch in Kerr County, with 66,000 acres; the South Fork Ranch in Kerr, Bandera, and Real counties, 94,000 acres; the Cottonwood Ranch in Kerr and Gillespie counties, 20,000 acres; the Y.O. Ranch in Kerr and Edwards counties, 56,000 acres; Paint Creek Ranch in Kimble and Edwards counties, 42,000 acres; the James River Ranch, Kimble and Mason counties, 60,000 acres; the Paint Rock Ranch in Kimble, Edwards, and Sut-

SHEEPSHEARING BARN

Sheep ranchers from fifty miles around herded their sheep to this barn each year in the spring to meet with the sheepshearers up from the border. Each rancher carried his own special token, which he gave the shearer for each of his own sheep sheared. When all the herds were finished, each shearer was paid by the owner according to the number of tokens he turned in. Before the shearers left the ranch, they wrote their names on the low rafters of the barn and usually added the year. The earliest date was 1899.

Just visible at the rear to the far right of the painting is the roof of a connecting barn, which held enough sheep to supply a day's work to the shearers. This allowed the shearing to continue even in rainy weather. The wool was then stored on the second level of the barn until it was taken to market.

LONE OAK: THE OLD HEADQUARTERS

In the early part of this century, Walter Schreiner, son of Capt. Charles Schreiner, moved here to Lone Oak and ran the ranch for many years. In addition to the main house (center) the complex consisted of barns, numerous bungalows for cowboys' families, a rock jail (left of painting), and a one-room schoolhouse.

Today the Longhorns run free among the abandoned structures. Walter's son, Charles Schreiner III, who has a great feeling for ranching heritage, collected Longhorn stock from around the country. He raised them into a magnificent herd and led in founding the Texas Longhorn Breeder's Association.

ton counties, 80,000 acres; and the Red Hole Ranch in Kimble and Gillespie counties, 30,000 acres. In addition, he held a half interest in the Crouch Ranch in Frio county, with 33,000 acres, and a half interest in the Prince Ranch in McMullen County, with 15,000 acres. His holdings also included the Southern Pacific lands in Presidio County, with 30,000 acres; the Skelp Creek Ranch in Menard County, 15,000 acres, and the R. B. Allen Ranch in Kimble County, 25,000 acres. At that time the Schreiner holdings totaled well over half a million acres.

In 1903 Walter Schreiner, one of the founder's sons, took up the life of a cowboy on the James River and later moved to the Live Oak Ranch. In 1907 he was working on the Y.O. He and his wife, Myrtle Barton, ran the Y.O. for many years. After Walter died, Myrtle, who had not been active in managing the ranch, assumed control and is generally credited with running a quality operation. Mac Hyde, son of a long-time Schreiner associate, served as manager during much of this time. Myrtle married twice more, once to Freeman W. Burford, and then to Dyke Cullum.

The ranch has suffered through hard times and has shrunk to around fifty thousand acres. One of the reasons for this plight is the fact that no oil has been discovered on Y.O. lands. Some lease money has been gained over the years, but the oil production that has been so beneficial to such spreads as the Waggoner, the Four Sixes, and the King was not available to the Schreiners. The mercantile business, more than once, rescued the Schreiners from bankruptcy, and the reliance on sheep and goats rather than cattle has often been the margin of their success. During the terrible drought of the 1950s, however, the Schreiners moved their herds to Montana in order to pull the animals through.

Several efforts have been made to establish profitable undertakings on the Y.O. One of these includes the stocking of exotic game for preservation purposes as well as for hunting. The Y.O. constitutes the largest exotic wildlife refuge in the United States. Game on the ranch include black buck antelope from India, Père David deer from China, scimitar horned onyx and addax from Chad, and barasingha deer from India and Nepal. In all, some forty species of exotics are on the ranch. Guided hunts have been available since the 1930s for native game and since the early 1960s for exotics. The prices are high, but, as someone noted, that is still cheaper than mounting a safari to the native habitat of these beautiful exotic animals.

The Y.O., and Charles Schreiner III, in particular, helped bring the Texas Longhorn back from the verge of extinction. Schreiner had been inspired by these cattle and other exotic wild game on the ranch belonging to his Uncle Louis, whom he had often visited as a boy near Kerrville. He also knew that the Y.O. existed principally because of the hardiness of the Longhorns his father and others had driven north to markets in Kansas. He felt that because of their heritage and their hardiness they were worth saving. In 1955, he bought six Longhorn calves and one young bull from the Wichita Mountain Wildlife Refuge near Lawton, Oklahoma, home of some of the few remaining original stock. Later in the 1950s, he bought some calves from Graves Peeler, an old-time cowman and brand inspector in South Texas. Those cattle he ran on a ranch in McMullin County. These efforts prospered and in the mid-1960s Schreiner began the Texas Longhorn Breeder's Association, which undertook the registration of Longhorn stock. Thirty charter members began the group, which now numbers more than three thousand. The projected headquarters of the Longhorn Association is in Fort Worth next to the world's largest honky-tonk, Billy Bob's Texas, in the old Stockyard District. The site stands vacant at the present time, however, except for a heroic-size statue of trail hands pushing seven Longhorn steers up the trail. Each of these steers represents, through brands on the animals, ranches from that early era: Peeler, Yates, Wright, Phillips, Butler, Marks, and the Wichita Mountain Refuge in Oklahoma.

82

This beautiful piece by sculptor Terry Kelsey is ample reminder of the heritage of the Longhorn as it affects Texas. Other kinds of cattle have been run on the ranch, especially Herefords, but now only Longhorns stock the ranch along with the game animals.

The most controversial, and therefore interesting, figure in the Schreiner story is Charles Schreiner III. A graduate of the University of Texas, he has been a flamboyant and colorful figure. Along with his equally colorful Kerrville friend, the late cartoonist Ace Reid, Charlie III, as he is known by thousands of people, has attracted a significant amount of attention. One of his activities was a trail drive of Longhorn cattle from San Antonio to Dodge City, Kansas, in 1966. The idea was conceived in a conversation among Ace Reid, Charlie III, and Stanley Frank, publisher of the *Livestock Weekly* of San Angelo, as they sat in the Inn of the Hills, a fine resort hotel in Kerrville. Schreiner was particularly pleased to push the drive because it would call attention to the hardiness of the Longhorn cattle and the Breeder's Association. The drive with its myriad details proved significantly different from those drives one hundred years earlier had, and when the herd left the portable pens at the Ramada Inn in San Antonio, many people doubted that it would ever reach its destination. The group drove the cattle by day but hauled the animals at night and thereby cut the length of time needed to complete the drive significantly. Included were a hundred steers, a hundred cowboys, and a hundred horses with all of the supplies and materials that had to accompany them. The commemorative drive crossed the Red River at historic Doan's Crossing, where Charlie III had arranged for a band of Indians, actually Anglo members of a sheriff's posse from Quanah disguised as nomadic raiders, to be there to demonstrate the kind of activity that Indians undertook in those days. Schreiner intended that the band of Indians ride up to the herd, demand an animal as their share for permission to cross Indian land, and drive it away. Instead, the band

charged the herd, scattered the cattle, caused cowboys to be unseated from horses, and dragged some from their horses, all much to the delight of the thousands of people gathered to watch the historic event. When the herd reached Kansas, the state's governor, William H. Avery, and Kenny House, a federal marshal who is a friend of Schreiner, were there to meet the herd.

Again in 1976, during the bicentennial of the United States, Charlie III undertook, at the request of the Chairman of the Board of Regents of Texas Tech University, to drive a small herd of Longhorns to Lubbock to herald the opening of the Ranching Heritage Center. The herd moved from San Antonio to Kerrville, San Angelo, Big Spring, and on to Lubbock. Since that time other trail drives have been held. In 1989, the Neiman-Marcus Christmas catalog, that high-water mark of Texas chic, advertised a Y.O. adventure in trail driving. One hundred and fifty spots on a trail drive to be held in early May of 1990 were sold at $767.00 per person. The offer sold out in two hours when the catalog was released on October 18. Two hundred seventy-five people rode out the main gate the first day. Each person was allowed to work as a trail hand on horseback, to sleep on the ground, to eat chuck wagon food, and to endure the heat and dust of the activity. The event was a roaring success.

The Schreiner home on the Y.O. Ranch is a two-story, limestone structure of seven thousand square feet, furnished with oriental, Victorian, and western motifs. It includes, as well, Charlie III's well-known gun collection in a specially constructed room-size vault with numerous memorabilia and a bar along with part of his book collection.

Charlie III has four sons, Charlie IV, Walter, Gus, and Louis. Three of the sons graduated from the University of Texas, but three also attended the Texas Christian University Ranch Management School. Charlie IV, who has been in charge of the ranch in the past, now sees after development. Walter is in charge of the Longhorn herd, and Louis oversees the hunting of game. The family also has youth camps and other kinds of activities. Motel-type facilities near the cookhouse can accommodate thirty-two people, and almost a hundred people can eat in the cookhouse. From fifteen to twenty thousand people visit the ranch each year. About five hundred of these are hunters. The others simply tour the ranch or take the photographic tour. Today the ranch runs about a thousand head of Longhorns on its fifty thousand acres. The sheep and goats that once populated the ranges have been eliminated because of loss to eagles and coyotes. Roundups these days are held by cowboys and, since 1970, without the aid of a helicopter. Remembered by Charlie III are roundups in the 1940s and 1950s, when the ranch still ran a wagon and cowboys stayed out for long periods of time. In those days, they had lots of good cowboys, many of them of Mexican extraction, and excellent ropers. Now the ranch has only five or six cowboys and keeps between fifty and sixty head of horses. One of the famous stallions on the ranch was Del Rio Joe, a cut-

ting horse Charlie III's mother bought for him in 1941. The ranch raised cutting horses until 1985.

The family also invested in the Y.O. Ranch Hilton, a two-hundred-room hotel, just off Interstate 10, in Kerrville. Currently the hotel is being operated by persons other than the Schreiner family. The decor of the Y.O. Ranch Hilton is unique indeed. The numerous game heads that hang around the walls of the lobby cause visitors to gawk for hours; the unique chandeliers composed of hundreds of branding irons must represent one of the most exotic items used in decor anywhere in the state. Even the bar in the swimming pool offers a unique opportunity for swimmers to sit in the water on the barstool, enjoying something cool.

Few other ranches and families have been so in the news socially. Mainly through the activities of Charlie III, Y.O. has done exotic things in exotic ways, commercial in nature, and has managed to hold on through what has been a trying time for one of the most famous brands in the West.

Y·O RANCH

84

Yturria Ranch

Willacy County Northwest of Brownsville

Ranching in South Texas can be traced back to the vast amounts of land provided by the King of Spain in the form of land grants, and it is there that the heritage of the Yturria Ranch begins.

Following the initial colonizing expeditions and the mapping of the region by José de Escandón in the mid 1700s, settlers moved to various communities being strategically established along the Rio Grande and its tributaries. These villages included Camargo, Mier, Reynosa, and, eventually, two locations on the north banks known as Dolores and Laredo.

After ten years of colonization, the King of Spain began to issue land grants to individuals who had been living within the communities for a prescribed amount of time and who now wished to privately own land. This resulted in an often bewildering variety of grants that included the long, thin *porciones*, which touched at the river for less than a mile and then extended north into the scrubland for up to eighteen miles. In addition, there were very large grants that covered tens of thousands of acres.

When Mexico won its independence from Spain, virtually all of the land grants were held to be valid, and, in fact, Mexico soon began issuing its own grants. Later, when Texas became a republic following its revolution, the Bourland-Miller Commission investigated the ownership of land in the South Texas region with an eye toward declaring the legality of the existing grants. Nearly all of the Spanish and Mexican land grants were judged to be valid, and the few that were rejected seemed to reflect the original intentions of the grants in regards to ensuring the presence of public or "common" land.

The Yturria Ranch is one of the few ranches in South Texas that has kept its identity through the various changes that have taken place over the last 175 years. Time and generations have seen the larger ranches broken up into smaller entities, which for the most part no longer remain in the hands of the original families. That is not the case of the Yturria Ranch.

The ranch was established near present-day Raymondville, several miles north of Brownsville, in the 1870s by Francisco Yturria. He was born October 4, 1830, in Matamoros, Mexico, a town just across the river from present-day Brownsville. His father was Col. Manuel María Yturria, a professional soldier, who first served in the Spanish army in Mexico and, after independence, in 1821, the Mexican army.

At the age of eighteen, Francisco Yturria moved from Matamoros to Brownsville to become an apprentice and store clerk for Charles Stillman. A bright young man, Yturria soon found favor with Stillman as well as with Stillman's partners, Richard King and Mifflin Kenedy, two men who would later become well known for their ranching interests. Stillman was an influential merchant who had been instrumental in founding Brownsville in the early 1850s through the establishment of a townsite company. In the beginning years of their partnership, however, Stillman, King, and Kenedy focused much of their attention on steamboats on the Rio Grande.

On December 23, 1853, Yturria married Felicitas Treviño, daughter of José Ygnacio Treviño, original grantee of the San Martin Grant as well as various *porciones* along the Rio Grande in the region that would later become Starr County. Her interest in these lands consisted of some forty thousand acres. Yturria's wife inherited these properties from her father, and Yturria bought out the interests of his wife's sister and brother and eventually controlled all of the original Treviño family tracts of land.

Yturria's business sense led him to open Texas' first private bank south of San Antonio in 1858. It was during this time that his empire spread from the mercantile business into ranching. In 1858 he also registered his brand consisting of a *Y* with a Spanish Christian cross inserted in it.

The brand is still in use today by Frank Yturria, a great-grandson.

Yturria was witness to the so-called Cortina War when, in September of 1859, Juan Cortina staged a raid across the river into Brownsville. Cortina was a controversial character who has been called by various people a hero, a thief, a bandit, an opportunist, and a revolutionary. Cortina raided Brownsville in retaliation for perceived injustices, and his men killed or wounded several citizens.

The unrest continued for quite some time, and Yturria commanded a militia unit to help repel the raids. Col. John Salmon "Rip" Ford, a well-known Texas Ranger, brought in a number of men and crossed into Mexico more than once in an attempt to stifle Cortina. Ford recounts in his memoirs that Yturria's action helped prevent Cortina from overcoming Brownsville and occupying the area.

Yturria prospered during the years of the American Civil War. Brownsville and South Texas were extremely important to the Confederacy during those years, for the costal waters became the backdoor for the South in an attempt to foil the Union blockade. Cotton could be shipped to Brownsville by land, taken across the river to Mexico, and shipped out from the Mexican port of Bagdad.

During the years of the Civil War, Mexico's situation was highly unstable. France invaded and put Maximilian on the throne of Mexico, and Yturria aligned himself with the French. Among the Yturria family papers can be found the document signed by Emperor Maximilian of Mexico bestowing the Knight of the Order of Guadalupe on Franciso Yturria. As a result of his allegiance to Maximilian, Yturria was appointed customs collector on the Mexican side of the river, and his position allowed him to determine what could and could not cross the river. As a result of this and his affiliation with Stillman, King, and Kenedy, he was able to participate in a virtual monopoly on river traffic. As a result, these men became extremely wealthy and powerful, and much of the cotton and supplies sent out from Bagdad found their way not only to European ports but also back up along the eastern seaboard where they were sold to the Union.

Following the Civil War and the collapse of the French regime in Mexico, Francisco Yturria was forced to flee, first to Cuba and then to France, where he learned that the Mexican government had issued orders to arrest him on a charge of treason. In addition, the victorious Union forces also sought him because of his alignment with the Confederacy. Yturria was forced to stay in exile for two years, during which time he entrusted his business concerns to his two brothers.

Eventually, Yturria received a pardon from Andrew Johnson, and the current generation of his family still has the original document in its possession. Yturria would also receive a full pardon from the Mexican government when Porfirio Díaz became president of Mexico. As a matter of fact, Díaz plotted his revolution from Brownsville and, during this time, stayed as a guest in Yturria's home.

When Yturria was able to return to Brownsville, he found that Stillman had moved back to his native New York while King and Kenedy had established their vast ranching centers near the present-day town of Kingsville. This left Brownsville with its rich river traffic still under the control of Francisco Yturria and others.

In 1870 Yturria purchased Punta del Monte (point of the brush), a ranch some fifty-five miles north of Brownsville. The ranch's name came from the fact that a heavy mesquite brush line had encroached up to that point. At the turn of the century, Yturria hired Walter Doughty, a well-known stockman in the area, to build a ranch headquarters. The buildings still stand on land owned by descendants and consist of a large house for the owner and an additional house for the manager, a chapel and schoolhouse, barns, supply sheds, a cookhouse, tool sheds, and other structures. At the time of Yturria's death on June 15 1912, he controlled approximately 200,000 acres that were the grazing lands for ten thousand head of cattle, five hundred head of horses and mules, and five hundred goats.

Over the years, family members have divided the land as the older generation passed on. Following the death of Francisco Yturria, his son, Daniel Yturria, and daughter, Isabel Yturria Garcia, received equal portions of the land. The property that went to the Garcia side has undergone several divisions, while Daniel Yturria's two sons, Fausto, Sr., and Herminio Yturria, received one-half of the property, which they divided equally.

As of 1991, all of the original lands are still owned by direct descendants of Francisco Yturria, a very unique situation in the history of South Texas ranching where, more often than not, the holdings were slowly broken down and the original identity of the ranch dissolved as land was sold. The largest part of the original Yturria Ranch, some 32,500 acres, is controlled by Frank Yturria, his brother Fausto, Jr., and his sister, Marion y Kimbro. In addition, Frank Yturria has added over 7,000 acres to the share he inherited from his father, Fausto Yturria, Sr.

This agriculturally rich section of the Rio Grande Valley teems with wildlife. Game animals on the ranch include deer, turkey, feral hogs, javelinas, ocelots, and the imported nilgai antelope, known as the blue bull of India. These large antelope are an exotic game animal imported by the King Ranch in the 1930s and have found a highly suitable habitat in the region—almost to the point of becoming a pest. This is the only animal hunted commercially on the Yturria Ranch.

Farming in this region has taken over some of the acres formerly grazed by livestock. On the Yturria Ranch, some three thousand acres are devoted to dry land farming of cotton, grain sorghum, and corn. The other acres are still devoted to cattle run by Frank Yturria. His herd consists principally of Santa Gertrudis cattle, but some Beefmaster blood has been introduced into the herd. These high-blooded animals have replaced the original Longhorn cattle that once roamed the ranges.

Frank Yturria has maintained considerable interest in fine horseflesh as well, and through his ties with the King and Kleberg families from the King Ranch, he has improved the original horse herd. One notable link is the gift by Robert Kleberg, Jr., to Fausto Yturria, Sr. (Frank's father), of Wimpy, Jr., a fine Quarter Horse stallion from one of the most famous King Ranch bloodlines. Today, Frank Yturria has racing Quarter Horses, a mixture of Quarter Horse and Thoroughbred blood. When Wimpy, Jr., died in 1970, he was replaced by a Thoroughbred stallion, the son of Tom Fool, the Kentucky Derby winner. This stallion sired the foals for the Yturrias until his death in 1990 at the age of 24. Since that time, a few select mares have been bred to outside stallions.

For the most part, horses on the Yturria Ranch are used for ranch work, and each cowboy is allocated five horses to carry out his duties. The men on the ranch, referred to variously as cowboys and vaqueros, are married men who live in houses on the ranch. The foreman, Johnny Posas, is related to the generations of vaqueros who have worked on the King Ranch. One employee of twenty-seven years, Oscar Garcia, still cowboys on the Yturria Ranch. The Mexican heritage of this ranch is a proud one, and Spanish is the working language on the range.

Roundups are demanding in the brush for cowboys on horseback. In recent years, the helicopter was tried but has come to be used less and less, especially during times of drought. It is far less expensive to trap the cattle in order to work them. This is accomplished by using *puertas matreras*, a device that allows the cattle to push their way into a small fenced pasture where water is found but then prohibits them from leaving again. This trapping method takes

THE BUNKHOUSE AT THE SAN FRANCISCO RANCH

Still standing and carefully restored by the owner, Dr. Frank Yturria, this bunkhouse was built by hands from the King Ranch. It is Sunday, a day of rest, and the cowboys are taking this opportunity to scrub clothes, do a little cleaning up, and sit around swapping stories. Some have begun barbecuing a hindquarter. The pit is dug, coals are hot, and some prickly pear cactus has been thrown in to make the coals smoke. The hindquarter, wrapped in burlap sacks, is being lowered on top of the coals and some corrugated tin placed over the hole. It will be good eating tonight. The room on the left with the chimney is the kitchen and used for everyday cooking. The room on the right is for sleeping, sometimes in a bunk and sometimes in a bedroll on the floor.

"PUNTA DEL MONTE"
YTURRIA RANCH

PUNTA DEL MONTE

Around the turn of the century, Walter Doughty was commissioned by Francisco Yturria to begin building ranch homes and other structures seen here. If one had visited the ranch in the early 1920s it would have looked very much this way. But in 1933, a hurricane ripped off many of the roofs of the buildings and destroyed the barn and the lookout tower that stood in the middle of the compound. The barn was located just beyond the border of the painting to the left. The buildings that can be seen are (from left to right) tool house, meat house (with sides of vertical separated slats to let in air and keep out animals), the tower, the commissary with bars on the windows, and a small part of the barn built to house some "Missouri Jack" mules. The largest house (just to the left of center) is the main or owner's house, the upper rooms kept ready for Yturria family visits. It wasn't until after World War II, after restoration from the hurricane damage, that the family maintained permanent residence there. To the right of the main house is the overseer's house and then the chapel, which was used as a school for the cowboys' children during the week and for Catholic mass on Sundays. Mass is still celebrated there today. Beyond the water tanks to the right and beyond the painting is a swimming hole formerly used by the cowboys for bathing. Six bungalows for cowboys' families are situated around the compound, some of which can be seen in the far background of the painting. Some of the trees around the two large homes still stand, but the white picket fence has been replaced by a rustic rail fence. The panorama of this ranch is a beauty to behold as one approaches it on the road running between two small lakes.

two or three days to capture a herd. A few mavericks that stay out longer by getting moisture from eating prickly pear are simply roped and sent to market as outlaws.

Working methods on this ranch consist mainly of simply putting the young calves in small pens and wrestling them down. This activity provides a family outing, especially for children on the ranch, and is viewed as great fun. The larger calves are roped by men on horseback.

The Mexican influence on gear is not noticeable on this ranch. The horsemen ride King Ranch saddles with traditional Texas lines—swelled forks, rolled cantles, double-rigging—and reflect other traits of the Anglo cowboy with felt hats in winter and straw hats in the summer. Their nylon lariat ropes are thirty feet in length, not the sixty-foot rawhide *reata* sometimes associated with Mexican culture and found in the hands of buckaroos in the northwestern United States. No plaited rawhide or twisted horse hair is used by the men. The horsemen wear long chaps and ride the medium-length tapaderos to protect themselves from the brush.

The brush in the region is, of course, an immense problem, and many ranchers have sought ways to cope with the mesquite, huisache, black brush, granjeno, and retama. Frank Yturria recounts that he fought the brush in traditional ways—chaining, dozing, root plowing, and reseeding—for a long time. In the last ten years, however, he has become conservation oriented and adopted a patchwork approach that allows him to take out heavy sections of brush but allows natural plants and grasses a chance to survive. In this way he maintains the ecological pattern of the area and retains the cover conducive to reproduction of game animals.

Another influence of the King Ranch is Yturria's commitment to the net wire fencing. This is erected on eight-foot long, six-inch top cedar posts, not the metal posts growing in popularity in some areas of the state, and forms all the fencing on the ranch.

Frank Yturria, the great-grandson of Francisco Yturria, is a gentleman in the old sense of the word. A retired air force officer and banker, Frank is a graduate of Texas A&M University and the University of the Phillipines. He plays polo, ranches, and serves his country. He served by appointment under President Ronald Reagan as U.S. representative to the South Pacific Commission. In 1989, President George Bush appointed him chairman of the Inter-American Foundation, where he oversees a large staff working for economic development in all Latin American and Caribbean countries.

He and his wife, Mary, are active in South Texas life. Both share a concern for preserving and presenting the unique heritage of South Texas and have contributed time, energy, and finances to the historic Brownsville museum. Frank's proud heritage represents the original spirit of ranching in the state of Texas. The activities of this family with their ranching as well as other varied interests continue to symbolize the influence and spirit that brought the ranching culture and tradition to the state.

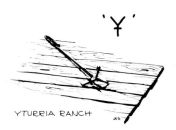

YTURRIA RANCH

Bibliography

Books and Articles

Adams, Lean Cox. "Winning Hand: Burk Burnett of the 6666 Ranch." Master's thesis, Texas Christian University, 1969.

Atherton, Lewis Eldon. *The Cattle Kings*. Bloomington: Indiana University Press, 1961.

Barrett, Neal, Jr. *Long Days and Short Nights: A Century of Ranching on the Y-O, 1880–1980*. Mountain Home, Tex.: Y-O Press, 1980.

Bolt, Richard. *Forty Years behind the Lid*. Privately printed, 1973.

Carmack, George. "Ranch History Straddles Border along Rio Grande." *San Antonio Express-News*, May 10, 1986, pp. 1L, 14L, 15L.

Casey, Clifford B. *Mirages, Mysteries, and Reality: Brewster County, Texas, of the Big Bend of the Rio Grande*. Hereford, Tex.: Pioneer Book Publishing, 1972.

Chapman, Art. "Catalog Cowboys." *Fort Worth Star-Telegram*, May 6, 1990, sec. 6, pp. 1, 11.

Clarke, Mary Whatley. "Broomtail Horses Build Cattle Empire." *Cattleman Magazine* 36, no. 8 (January 1950): 25, 81–82, 84, 86, 88–89.

————. *A Century of the Cow Business: A History of the Texas and Southwestern Cattle Raisers Association*. Fort Worth: Texas and Southwestern Cattle Raisers Association, 1976.

————. "John Biggs: Three D Ranch Manager." *Cattleman Magazine* 49, no. 10 (March 1963): 50–54.

————. *The Swenson Saga and the SMS Ranches*. Austin: Jenkins Publishing Company, 1976.

Clayton, Lawrence. *Watkins Reynolds Matthews: A Biography*. Abilene, Tex.: Hardin-Simmons University Press, 1989.

————. "Watt Matthews: Historical Preserver." *Heritage Magazine* 4, no. 3 (1986), 30–31.

Denhardt, Robert Moorman. *The King Ranch Quarter Horses*. Norman: University of Oklahoma Press, 1970.

Dobie, J. Frank. *Cow People*. 1964; rpt. Austin: University of Texas Press, 1984.

Douglas, C. L. *Cattle Kings of Texas*. 1939; rpt. Austin: State House Books, 1989.

Duke, Cordia Sloan, and Joe B. Frantz. *6000 Miles of Fence: Life on the XIT Ranch of Texas*. Austin: University of Texas Press, 1961.

Durham, George, and Clyde Wantland. *Taming the Nueces Strip*. Austin: University of Texas Press, 1962.

Ennis, Michael. "Four Sixes Ranch: Renewed Vigor for a Cattle Baron's Historic West Texas Mansion." *Architectural Digest*, June 1992, pp. 180–186.

Ford, John Salmon. *Rip Ford's Texas*. Edited by Stephen B. Oates. Austin: University of Texas Press, 1963.

Goodwyn, Frank. *Life on the King Ranch*. New York: Crowell, 1951.

Haley, J. Evetts. *Charles Schreiner General Merchandise: The Story of a Country Store*. Kerrville, Tex.: Charles Schreiner Company, 1969.

————. *The Heraldry of the Range*. Illustrated by H. D. Bugbee. Canyon, Tex.: Panhandle Plains Historical Society, 1949.

————. *The XIT of Texas and the Early Days of the Llano Estacado*. 2d ed. Norman: University of Oklahoma Press, 1953.

Halsell, H. H. *Cowboys and Cattleland*. Nashville, Tenn.: Partheon Press, n.d.

Hancock, William C., and Wylie W. Bennett, Sr. "Rancho Grande." *Frontier Times* 38, no. 2 (February–March 1964): 14–16, 49–54.

Harper, Minnie Timms, and George Dewey Harper. *Old Ranches*. Dallas: Dealey & Lowe, 1936.

Hastings, Frank. *A Ranchman's Recollections*. Austin: Texas State Historical Association, 1985.

Hendrix, John. *If I Can Do It Horseback: A Cow-Country Sketchbook*. Austin: University of Texas Press, 1964.

————. "Waggoner's Outfit." *Cattleman Magazine* 25, no. 6 (November 1938): 39–43.

Hessin, Sandra Swenson. "History of the SMS Ranches." *Persimmon Hill* 2, no. 3 (Winter 1972): 11–17.

History of the Cattlemen of Texas. Introduction by Harwood P. Hinton. 1914; rpt. Austin: Texas State Historical Association, 1991.

Hodge, Larry D., and Sally S. Victor. "The Legendary King Ranch." *Texas Highways Magazine* 38, no. 1 (January 1991): 4–11.

Holden, Frances Mayhugh. *Lambshead before Interwoven: A Texas Range Chronicle, 1848–1878*. College Station: Texas A&M University Press, 1982.

Holden, William Curry. *The Espuela Land and Cattle Company: A Study of a Foreign-Owned Ranch in Texas*. Austin: Texas State Historical Association, 1970.

Howard, Orville. "J. J. Gibson: Boss of the Four Sixes." *Cattleman Magazine* 72, no. 3 (August 1985): 48–50, 52, 54, 56, 58, 60.

"John Biggs New Manager of Waggoner Estate." *Cattleman Magazine* 39, no. 9 (February 1953): 110.

Kinard, Knox. *A History of the Waggoner Ranch*. Master's thesis, University of Texas, 1941.

King County: Windmills and Barbed Wire: Quanah, Tex.: Nortex Press, 1976.

King Ranch: 100 Years of Ranching. Corpus Christi: Corpus Christi Caller-Times, 1953.

Lea, Tom. *The King Ranch*. 2 vols. Boston: Little, Brown and Company, 1957.

Lincoln, John. *Rich Grass and Sweet Water: Ranch Life with the Koch-Matador Cattle Company*. College Station: Texas A&M University Press, 1989.

McCoy, Dorothy Abbott. *Texas Ranchmen: Twenty Texans Who Help Build Today's Cattle Industry*. Austin: Eakin, 1987.

Mackenzie, Murdo. "The Matador Ranch." *Panhandle-Plains Historical Review* 21 (1948): 94–95.

Matthews, Sallie Reynolds. *Interwoven: A Pioneer Chronicle*. 1936; rpt. 2d ed. El Paso: Carl Hertzog, 1958; rpt. 3d ed. Austin: University of Texas Press, 1973; rpt. 4th ed. College Station: Texas A&M University Press, 1982.

Mize, Richard. "Where the Buffalo Roamed." *Wichita Falls Time Record News*, August 14, 1990, p. 1B.

Murrah, David J. *The Pitchfork Land and Cattle Company: The First Century*. Lubbock: Texas Tech University Press, 1983.

Nixon, Jay. *Stewards of a Vision: A History of King Ranch*. Kingsville, Tex.: King Ranch, 1986.

Nordyke, Lewis. *Cattle Empire: The Fabulous Story of the 3,000,000 Acre XIT*. New York: William Morrow, 1949.

Pattie, Jane. "Leonard Stiles: The South Texas Brand." *Cattleman Magazine* 77, no. 8 (January 1991): 40, 41, 43, 45, 46, 48, 50, 52–54, 58; 77, no. 9 (February 1991): 45, 47, 49, 51–52, 54, 56.

Pearce, W. M. *The Matador Land and Cattle Company*. Norman: University of Oklahoma Press, 1964.

"Poco Bueno." *Cattleman Magazine* 43, no. 4 (September 1956): 157.

"Ranching by Helicopter." *Cattleman Magazine* 39, no. 12 (May 1953): 28–29, 96.

Reeves, Frank. "Horse Breeding by Selection." *Cattleman Magazine* 31, no. 4 (September 1944): 23–25, 102–103.

———. "Two of the Great Ones in Real Cattle and Horse Country." *Cattleman Magazine* 55, no. 4 (September 1968): 86–93.

———. "The Waggoner Story." *Cattleman Magazine* 56, no. 3 (August 1969): 48–49, 62, 64, 66.

Rister, Carl Coke. *Fort Griffin on the Texas Frontier*. Norman: University of Oklahoma Press, 1956.

———. *Robert E. Lee in Texas*. Norman: University of Oklahoma Press, 1946.

Sanders, Alvin H. *The Story of the Herefords*. Chicago: Breeder's Gazette Print, 1914.

SMS Ranches. Privately printed information pamphlet distributed by SMS Ranches. No date.

"SMS Ranches." In *Handbook of Texas*. Edited by Walter Prescott Webb et al. 2 vols. Austin: Texas State Historical Association, 1952.

Sonnichsen, C. L. *Cowboys and Cattle Kings Alive on the Range Today*. Norman: University of Oklahoma Press, 1950.

"Texas Trails." *San Antonio Light*, January 22, 1928, part 2, p. 2.

Walker, Peggy. *George Humphreys: 6666 Cowboy and Lawman*. Burnet, Tex.: Eakin, 1978.

Warnock, Barton H. *Wildflowers of the Davis Mountains and the Marathon Basin, Texas*. Photographs by Peter Koch. Alpine, Tex.: Sul Ross State University Press, 1977.

Williams, J. W. *The Big Ranch Country*. Wichita Falls, Tex.: Terry Brothers, 1954.

Young, Bell. *Sixty-five Years in the Cow Business in Texas, New Mexico, and Arizona*. 2d ed. Cisco, Tex.: Longhorn Press, 1961.

Interviews

Blakemore, William B., II. By Lawrence Clayton. June 17, 1991.

Burns, John. By Lawrence Clayton. Several between 1985 and 1989.

Green, Bill. By Lawrence and Sonja Clayton. January 23, 1991.

Green, Bob. By Lawrence and Sonja Clayton. January 23, 1991.

Lange, Aubrey. By Lawrence Clayton. Several between 1985 and 1989.

McLaury, Buster. By Lawrence and Sonja Clayton. July 5, 1990, at Alanreed, Texas.

Mathis, Gary. By Lawrence Clayton. August 20, 1990.

Matthews, Watkins Reynolds. By Lawrence Clayton. Several between 1985 and 1989.

Moberly, Terry. By Lawrence Clayton. Several between 1985 and 1989.

Patterson, Jim. By Lawrence Clayton. August 14, 1990.

Peacock, Benny. By Lawrence Clayton. August 14, 1990.

Peacock, George. By Lawrence Clayton. Several between 1985 and 1989.

Schreiner, Charles, III. By Lawrence and Sonja Clayton. March 17, 1991.

Smith, Billy. By Lawrence Clayton. August 20, 1980.

Stevens, John. By Lawrence and Sonja Clayton. June 16, 1990.

Yturria, Frank. By Lawrence Clayton. March 13, 1991, by telephone.